THEY FOLLOWED
THE
GLORY TRAIL

by

Roberta H. Green

COPYRIGHT © 1987

ALL RIGHTS RESERVED

DEDICATION

To my family whose faith in me has never failed, and to the pioneers who have made these stories possible.

Cal Clawson discussing latest strike with old "Pike's Peak" friend, Sam Tripp, as Sam prepares to leave for the summer's prospecting.

TABLE OF CONTENTS

The Call of Gold	1
The Glory Trail	7
Bull-Whacker to Mayor	13
Sammy Holman "Hello"	19
Call Me Cowboy Joe	27
The Price Was A Bottle	31
Custer's First Lady	36
The Sturdy Oak	46
His Trademark Was A Diamond Hitch	59
The Swedish Sojourner	68
Child of Tragedy	79
Mary, Queen of Courage	88
Josie -- The Girl Whose Feet Trod The Paths to Gold and Silver Mines	96
The Badge of Courage	104
Horseback Medicine in Early Custer County	112
She Walked A Lonely Road	124
She Lived in God's Domain	134
If You Can See through The Mists	143

THE CALL OF GOLD

Calvin C. Clawson -- born at Lancester, Penn. 1840 -- died at his home between Custer and Bonanza, Idaho, May 15, 1911. What a brief statistic for the exciting life he led.

The story should jump out of print to convey the intensity and intoxication of associating with pathfinders, goldfinders and Indians. He journeyed with covered wagons. He knew Majors and Judges personally, as well as Representatives and Senators. He corresponded regularly with the President of the United States. People with great fortunes had him assay their nuggets and trusted him to make sales of their mining properties -- ranging in the hundreds of thousands of dollars.

He began his heady, turbulent life at the age of 12, when he apprenticed to a printer. Stories of the ever-changing broiling uproarious West, fascinated him He dreamed and worked for two years learning his trade. He must have been an avid student as the following recommendation testifies: Brownsville, Pa., November 9, 1854. It affords me great pleasure to recommend the bearer, Mr. Calvin C. Clawson, to the friendship and confidence of any gentlemen with whom he may seek employment. Having served a regular apprenticeship of two years in my establishment, and having been during much of that time and subsequently entrusted with the direction and affairs of the office, I can cheerfully testify to his capacity, integrity, faithfulness, and skill. It is with sincere regret I part with him and with his well-being and prosperity. If a courteous and modest demeanor, a kind and obliging disposition, and an unblemished moral character, can give him success or commend him the favor of the community, I feel assured of his good fortunes and of his enjoying to an eminent degree the good-will and regards of his fellowmen. Signed Robert W. Jones, publisher and proprietor of the Cumberland Presbyterian).

Cal attended college from age fourteen until sixteen and supported himself. At sixteen when he could no longer stand the thought of all the great things happening in the West, he wrote home to his mother that he had an offer on a newspaper in LeCompton, the turbulent capitol of Kansas Territory. He was on his way. He had been the man of the family since he was twelve, when his father died and now he felt his mother could manage without his support.

After working on the LeCompton paper for a year, he was offered a better job on a paper in Monial, Wisconsin, and left for that town. While working in Wisconsin he fell in love with one of the most refined and socially accepted young ladies of this town, Czarina Llewellyn.

She was small and dainty. Since her family placed a great deal of emphasis on education, she had the rare privilege of attending college, graduating when she was seventeen years old.

They met at a church gathering and after a swift courtship were married April 26, 1858-- both were eighteen years old. As they were both interested in history in the making and were well-read on current events, it seemed only natural that she would also become entranced with all the excitement of the goldstrikes and the wild fever of going West. In the spring of 1859, they made the journey by boat and ox team to the new gold fields of "Pikes Peak," the name by which the country around Denver was then known.

Since everyone could not leave their commitments behind and take off for the goldfields, the paper where Cal worked made him promise to send back reports to them. He had packed his tools and small hand press and the following copy was duly recorded, and copied from Mrs. Clawson's scrapbook entitled, "In A Camp near Omaha City, May 18, 1859."

"I promised to write you a line from this place and as we expect to leave here tomorrow morning and take up our march Peak-ward; I write now as the next mailing place will be Ft. Kearney, a two weeks travel. We are camped in a beautiful ravine about one mile north of Omaha City, in company with a good many others; in fact you can see tents and wagons in every direction, some pointed for California, some for the Pikes' Peak and not a few for home. You must not think either, that we are in a company of men alone, for as I write I see bright blue eyes peek from under bonnets, as angel's feet glide noiselessly by, while hoops flutter majestically in the wind. A company of Californians are camped along side of us, and they have quite a number of the fair sex with them, which makes things look more civilized.

The trip out was very pleasant although we were longer on the way than anticipated. We left Hannibel, on the Mississippi, at 10 o'clock on Thursday, and arrived in St. Joseph at 10 the same night -- a distance of 206 miles. I found Hannibel and St. Joseph railroads in much better condition than I had anticipated, being fairer than most of our Western roads.

We remained aboard the steamer St. Mary, at the St. Jo. wharf, till Saturday night before we headed for Omaha. From St. Jo. to Omaha the distance is 300 miles by river, and we were from Saturday night till Tuesday morning getting here. The river is very high and difficult to navigate on account of current -- boats not being able to make more than four or five miles per hour. At White Cloud, Nebraska I noticed hundreds of government teams loading with provisions for Utah, intended for troops, the contractors get 23 cents a pound for transporting freight to Salt Lake. I noticed at the same place a great many teams returning home from the gold country, most of them having been out for a week and also met a company of hand-carts returning with them to the states. One of the wagons had a sign on the side, 'Take the advice of a humbugged fool and go home to your farm.'

Last night was our first camping night, and the bright full moon came up slowly and made the long line of white ghostly looking tents a contrast with the tall trees. Some hearts were merry and some thought of friends left at home. Some were singing and I distinguished voices of both sexes floating on the breeze. Omaha is the prettiest place I have seen on the river. All kinds of business is carried on. The people here are of a different class from any I have met with in these new countries, kind obliging and not trying to 'shave' every newcomer. The Capitol building located on the hill near town would be an ornament to any state in the Union.

In every town along the river the streets were crowded with emigrants' wagons -- destination Pike's Peak. At St. Jo. I saw 14 teams go over on the ferry boat at once and the wharf had hundreds waiting. It surpasses anything on record.

In the fall of 1862, the Clawsons returned to Wisconsin, where their only child, a boy named Llewellyn, was born. In the spring of 1863 Calvin could not keep his wonderlust desires quieted and departed for new strikes in the Idaho Territory. Describing this phase of his life he says,

"Along with everyone else I stampeded to new discoveries, prospected old one, dived for 'bedrock' and dug rim-rock -- in short gone crazy like everyone else.

I was in on the first discovery of Alder gulch (Virginia City). I was on the stampede and afterwards, interviewed at length one of the original discovery men (Harry Edgar). This was in '63 when I saw the camp come up. The history of Alder gulch discovery was found by accident. On an expedition into the Big Horn and Yellowstone country some men in the party were turned back by Crow Indians, and while on their return to Bannock, discovered Alder Gulch. The others of the party were followed by the Crows and some of them were massacred at night on the banks of the Big Horn. Sam L. Hauser (afterward Governor of Montana) was one of the party. I was not with them, but met some of them after the fight as they were getting out -- some of them badly wounded. In 1864 I was acquainted with one of the men who found the famous 'lost Chance' strike at Helena. I was there from the first, helped measure off claims, assisted at the first mine meetings to formulate the laws etc., and got my sluices set and running on the 16th day of August 1864, weeks before a cabin was put up. The first habitation was a tent and an alder 'shack' attachment or annex, which is quite a contrast to the Capitol buildings at the present.

I stayed for years in this section of the country, and not until 1870 did I move to Deer Lodge where my wife and son joined me. There I worked on the new 'Northwest' paper with Captain. J. H. Miles, who was the owner of the it. I was in the capacity of all round reporter and correspondent and also held a case when I wished to. I also learned to assay ore, as I felt it would come in handy."

Life in Deer lodge took on excitement for the Clawsons. They were in the heart of the country they both loved and were popular with people of education. They were much sought after, attending openings of grand operas, Masquerade balls, banquets for governors, concerts, lodges, and lectures. They counted Deer Lodge days as great memories. None of this social life deterred them when they heard of a new goldstrike at an out-of-the-way place called Custer, on the Yankee Fork of the Salmon river. Since Calvin wanted to be in on the first possible assaying and claim staking he left for Custer in the spring of 1879. Mrs. Clawson was left to dispose of what was necessary and followed the rest in the fall of 1880.

Custer had all the earmarks of other strikes they had attended. Tents were pitched haphazardly wherever a vacant spot could be found. Hardly any preparation was made for the below-zero weather and many miners lacked sufficient clothing to keep them from freezing. Consequently, many had to leave the first winter. Calvin had a cabin built at the mouth of Jordon Creek between Custer and Bonanza, on the main stage road. It again became the mecca of the educated people of the Yankee Fork. Cal and his wife subscribed to various newspapers and magazines and shared them with their neighbors. People came from towns around to view Mrs. Clawson's ore collection. She sketched and painted; helped young friends learn these skills. His assay office was in their home bringing many people, with their ore samples and high hopes to their door. Cal was district Recorder and Notary Public of that end of the county.

They spent some time in Boise, when Calvin represented Blaine County in the Idaho Legislature. They also spent a few winters in Challis, so they would be close to the Challis Hot Springs where they felt Mrs. Clawson might have some relief from the constant rheumatic pain which finally crippled her so badly she was confined to a wheelchair.

The ever-present gold-fever which Cal carried with him many years kept him on the Yankee Fork among crumbling buildings and many lost dreams. He was always looking for and hoping for another great strike, when his hills would come alive again.

In 1906 his beloved partner was freed from her battle with constant pain. Five years later his horse stumbled on a narrow trail and fell with him, causing an injury to his side from which he never recovered. Cal died in his beloved Yankee Fork country May 15, 1911.

Cal left the tools of his trade and an awesome record of papers he either worked on, managed or edited, from LeCompton and Menial, Wis. he had moved for a short time to Omaha and was associate editor of the Omaha Bee. In Idaho he had worked on The Ketchum Keystone, the Prospector (a paper published briefly on the Yankee Fork; had charge of The Yankee Fork Hearld. With the help of his wife, they had published it during the winter of 1879 and 1880. Later he worked on the Graphic, Boise Statesman, and The Idaho World. In addition he wrote for the "Challis Messenger" for thirty years under the name of "Graph."

A lasting tribute should be paid him as he was instrumental in having the Yellowstone Park put aside for a National Park. He was detailed, along with five other men, by the Governor of Montana to investigate this country and report its unique characteristics. After much correspondence with the Governor and H. Clagett, a member of Congress from Montana, Cal's pleas were so effective that Clagett put up the bill for the Yellowstone Park. It passed -- another accomplishment of a dedicated pioneer who followed the lure of gold from Montana to the Yankee Fork and lies with his wife among the ruins of Bonanza.

(Top LtoR) Cal and Czarina Clausen
(Bottom) Clausen Cabin; Lew and Cal.

THE GLORY TRAIL

Czarina Llewellyn Clawson -- born to pioneer. She came from pioneering stock and kept that tradition alive.

Her grandfather, Llewellyn, was born in central New York, in 1757, where a colony of Llewellyns from Wales had earlier settled. The family name, interpreted in their native language meant "The Lion's Enemy." Llewellyns had fought in the Continental Army in the Revolutionary War, to again be the Lion's enemy. At the close of the Revolution a few of the survivors of the original colony emigrated westward and settled in the beautiful valley of Monongalis, near what is now Morgontown, West Virginia. There Joseph Llewellyn was born, married a young lady named Lousia Fry, and fathered Czarina, their oldest child of seven -- four girls and three boys.

When Czarina was eight years old, they moved to Uniontown, Pennsylvania, and later to Monial, Wisconsin. The Llewellyns were highly intelligent people, numbering among their ancestors, doctors, lawyers, and successful businessmen. Czarina was fortunate in having parents who were far advanced for their times. They insisted their girls as well as their boys receive a proper education. They were helpful in selecting a college for young ladies, and she enrolled there, making very satisfactory marks. Czarina graduated in the spring of her seventeenth year. Her advisors gave her a recommendation to present to school boards which read,

> "This certifies that I have examined Miss Czarina Llewellyn, and so believe that she is qualified with regards to moral character, learning, and ability to teach common school in this town for one year from this date, Monroe, Wisconsin, November 26, 1857 -- Signed Adams Birthiff T. S. Principal I. B. Bachman."

So Miss Czarina Llewellyn applied for a school and was accepted. Her pay was $12.00 per month and board. For the first year, this was considered top wages and she recorded in her diary,

> "I am proud and happy to have so much respect accorded me. I consider the teaching profession one of the most rewarding and exciting professions I could have chosen."

One evening she was invited to a tea given by her girlfriends. When she entered the parlor, they were all chattering at once about the young new printer who had just signed on at the "Monial News."

He seemed so young to them to have such a responsible position, and they were also wondering how they could find the proper way to make his acquaintance. They finally agreed it would be convenient to have their mothers invite him to a church social that was scheduled for the following week As the time of the social drew near, great preparations were being made with lovely dresses and fancy hairstyles. The rivalry was fun; but when Calvin entered the room, he noticed the small, dainty, lady with the curls across her forehead. He liked what he saw and made his way through the crowd to meet her. He was not only taken with her appearance; but when he started a conversation he was pleasantly surprised to find she could keep up her end of the conversation. He was even surpassed on certain subjects. Needless to say, he was badly smitten that evening and courted Czarina as diligently as he had applied himself to getting an education. She invited him to meet her family. They were impressed with their daughter's selection and were happy to give them their blessing. On April 26, 1858 Czarina and Calvin were united in marriage.

During their courtship he had talked endlessly about the great goldstrikes of the west; so when he suggested they start making arrangements to go "West" she met his ideas with enthusiasm and eagerness. They planned the trip well, putting away all available monies and making clothing that would be durable for them on such a strenuous trip.

April 11, almost a year from the time they were married, they headed west. From her diary she says of the trip,

> "Left home and went to Omaha, where we took the steamer, 'Columbia' bound for Ft. Benton. When we arrived at Omaha we decided to celebrate our freedom from cares and worries and attended the theatre. About the trip we seemed to average about thirty miles a day on a good run. Windy and cold -- One day we tied up early, so we went out into the country and purchased some eggs and fresh milk. Pulled into Franklin where we paid our respects to Gov. Faulkand, the printer, Mr. Kingsbury. One day we tied up, and Cal and I visited the Indians and their Wigwams. Another day we went hunting and camped out all night. We killed an antelope and saw a lot of Indians. The folks on the boat thought we had been killed and the ladies shed tears of joy, at our appearance. Another day we saw a dead Indian, shot by a white man."

Her letters home were full of stories of Indians -- fortunes made and lost in one night at the poker tables -- of the way the miners and prospectors seem to care only for tomorrow and the big strike that would surely be theirs. Letters she received from home were cherished, and re-read many times. From a letter received from her mother July 6, 1858, "Dear Czarina, with my right-hand helper gone, home is not the same without your smiling face and willing hands -- I have not completed all of Anna's clothes for school yet, and she will be leaving soon. George and Willie go to school regularly. It only took your letter six days to travel here, what fast mail these days. We are all so afraid you will not be able to come home this fall and we miss you so much. Your father is sure you will not be able to come. Little George says he is going to save all his chickens until you come home, so you see, you will have to come. There have been many parties here, but none the same with you and Cal gone. Your father bought me a dress-length I will send you a piece of it. It is our favorite color, green. It will look well made up. He has also made Eva a very pretty lounge with a turned back and ends. She has covered the cushions with red and orange damask. I am going to have him make one for you like it, to have when you get back. It is getting late and I must say good night, from your affectionate mother, Lousia Llewellyn. P.S. Mr. Waddlow is holding a position open for Calvin. (George and Willie and Anna mentioned in the letter, brothers and sisters of Czarina -- George later became a very successful businessman, dealing in real estate and land exchange. Willie became Major W.H.H. Llewellyn of Las Crues, N.M., Commander of N.M. in Col. Roosevelt's regiment of Rough Riders in Cuba.)

And from a letter cherished in her possessions was found this letter from her little brother George:

> Monroe, February 24, 1861 -- Your letter was so long coming -- seventeen days, and we miss hearing from you so much. The snow is so deep this winter. I will tell you about it. It is three feet deep and drifted in some places until it is thirty feet deep. It is so deep the R.R. cars did not get in for three days, but last Sunday they came in and they were loaded with papers and letters, with yours included. There have been great parties here this winter. Overstreets had a party last week at McKees' new hall. The boys had to pay fifteen cents a piece and as I hadn't the money, I stayed home. Anna went with Daniel and danced until twelve o'clock. The next dance will be in honor of 'Ole Abe' taking his seat at the white house. We all felt very bad because you could not come home this spring. I want you to come early next fall and bring that pony you said you would bring back to me. I got a little cart that will be just right for him. Baby Charlie is looking at your picture and calling you 'Ena'. We have over a mile of ice on the river and the skating is as good as ever. Please come home and bring the pony. Your brother, George.

No doubt letters from home were a life-line to a world that was gone.

Finally her family was rewarded with a visit from the Clawsons, in the fall of 1862. While there, their only child, Llewellyn was born. Czarina was with them for much longer than a visit -- again Cal was badly bitten by the gold-fever. He knew he could not take a small child, on the rough prospecting trips he anticipated; so his wife and child lived with her parents for six years. When Cal was finally settled in Deer Lodge, Montana, Czarina and Lew joined him making the trip again by boat, ox team and railroad.

Life picked up momentum. They were invited to all social gatherings. She sewed fancy silk and velvet dresses; bought dancing shoes; called on ladies for afternoon teas; had visiting days "home;" and attended lectures, operas and balls.

One evening Cal came home bursting with exciting news of a new and better strike. His infectious enthusiasm soon had the Clawson home, torn from everyday matters. This strike was in a little-known-place called Bonanza in the heart of Idaho. Instantly there was no more interest in Lodge lectures, mostly their interest was in newspapers. All interest centered on the new strike.

Idaho became their home. A four room cabin was built with love and care. (It withstood the elements, but when the dredge was operating in the Yankee Fork the owners believed it would work its way as far as the cabin; so they had the cabin torn down.)

Even here in a raw mining town Czarina's deep and abiding love of learning kept her interested in the many facets of the mining industry. While in Deer Lodge she had started a collection of ore samples from all the great strikes of the west. She continued to add to this collection. It became so renowned and was considered so valuable, that she was appointed by Gov. Wills, one of two commissioners from Custer County, to take her fine cabinet of ores to the World's Fair at Chicago.

She had also taken up oil painting while in Deer Lodge, receiving lessons from an excellent instructor, and had begun to write stories. Through the years she was a correspondent for Omaha Republican, Butte Miner, Challis Messenger, Ketchum Keystone, and Eastern papers. She also wrote sketches of Upper Salmon River, Wood River, and the Sawtooth countries, illustrating them at times.

Calvin never struck it rich -- only in friendships and trusts and in the love of a wife whose knowledge and interest kept them friends as well as lovers.

Twelve years before her death Czarina had a severe illness from which she never fully recovered. Medical aid, change of altitude, and a journey to New Mexico and Los Angeles brought no relief. Seven years after returning to her mountain home spinal infection became permanent with loss of strength in the lower limbs.

Cal and Lew prospected a claim they had on Dicken Mountain and were only able to work it during the summer months. They never considered leaving Czarina down in the valley, but built her a beautiful little cabin high on the mountain -- making the doorway extra wide to accommodate her wheelchair. They fashioned a veranda 10'x20' feet across the front and a balustrade enclosing the edges so she could manipulate her wheelchair out to see the mountains, valleys, and place she had climbed searching for fossils and artifacts.

While her menfolk were away working, she entertained herself by pushing her chair onto the veranda, studying the mountain scene before her; and then she painted that scene on the unbleached lining across one wall of the cabin. It would have been lasting testimony of her ability to convey the mountains she loved to a picture, but time and rats ruined her last painting.

Her strength finally faded, and she died at the family home at the mouth of Jordon Creek, February 14, 1905. Funeral services were held in the Miner's hall at Custer. The Sunday School class sang the hymns and her pioneer friends carefully lowered her body into the grave.

The long journey down the "Glory Trail" from far away West Virginia, ended in the little cemetery in Bonanza, Idaho.

Czarina Clawson

One of the Balls the Clawsons attended in Deer Lodge.

SECOND FANCY DRESS AND Masquerade Ball.

WEDNESDAY EVENING, APRIL 12TH, 1871.

☞ At the request of many citizens who did not participate [and all of those who did], I will give a second

MASQUERADE AND FANCY DRESS

Party at Stuart Hall, Deer Lodge, on the above date. I have procured an extra supply of Costumes, engaged the best Music, and shall spare no pains to make everything as enjoyable as possible.

With these arrangements, the universal desire for a second Masquerade is a guarantee that it will be in all respects a splendid success.

Tickets, Five Dollars.

SUPPER [extra] will be furnished in the lower Hall. The Committees will be announced in the papers of this week. ☞ No improper characters will be admitted. Apply for

Costumes at the Hall.

JOHN O'NEILL, 404.

"New North-West" Print.

BULL-WHACKER TO MAYOR

Alexander Topance began his wheeling, dealing career at age seven, while sailing with his family from Harve, France to New York in 1846. The drinking water was rancid, and so he helped himself to a plug of tobacco from his father's pouch and traded it for some water that was palatable. From this early start he developed the character that later built roads, bought ranches and dealt in fortunes.

It caused him to be dissatisfied with homelife. Therefore, he left home for the West when he was ten years old. He lived with freighters, (who were lonely men) cowboys, families, and generally found a way to earn a mealticket. Meanwhile he observed all new jobs and opportunities around him. At age fifteen he had learned to be a bull-whacker. he served sometime with a freight line in their service. Then he tried the wilder life of a Pony Express rider; and my 1857 was serving as an assistant wagon master for the military forces under Albert Sidney Johnson in the so-called, "Mormon War." From there he scented the money to be had around the gold fields and hit the trail for Colorado in 1860.

He was different from most of the young men; his dream did come true. He struck a rich vein, and made a quick fortune of $20,000, and saw it swindle to nothing when he used it to purchase worthless claims. He struggled to salvage something, and sold the last of all his holdings there in the fall of 1962 for two mules, two horses, a wagon, some food and supplies. Like all the rest, he still had a lesson to learn.

When he heard of a new strike in Montana he headed in that direction. On February 2, 1863, one hundred and sixty three men and one woman started for those goldfields of Virginia City. Alexander Topance, at the age of 23, was their leader. Many places on their journey they traveled through snow four feet deep; the weather was bitterly cold with many people suffering from frosted hands and feet.

When their party sighted Fort Hall they also sighted a wagon train surrounded by Indians. (The besieged people later told them they had stood off the Indians for eight days.) When the Indians saw the reinforcements, they fell back, but kept in sight and followed the combined train day and night for the rest of the trip.

The first night they threw a great celebration in honor of the rescue. Each wagon contributed a portion of food. The men pulled the wagon covers off the wagons, and stretched them tightly on the ground for a dance floor. Everyone participated in the good times, eating, drinking and dancing into the early morning.

The next day, jubilant, but tired the combined train started on the last stretch of the journey up the Snake River to Camas Creek over the continental divide to Horse Prairie. From there they arrived at Bannock City, Montana, May 14, 1863 -- a total of 120 days.

Freighting on the frontier was good business. Alexander lost no time taking advantage of this. He went to Utah and gathered together eggs from all over the area paying a penny an egg. Then he sold them at a profit of $2.00 per dozen. He also purchased a pig weighing over 600 pounds, for $12.00, freighted it to Utah, where he received $1.00 per pound. He bought and sold everything and anything to turn a profit.

Eventually he went into the cow business at a place near Chesterfield, renting 2800 square miles of land for $2500 per year. He and his partner had 10,000 head of cattle and 26,000 sheep.

This life proved too boring for him. When he heard of a goldstrike and roads to be built, he sold his interest in the ranch plus the cattle and sheep, but retained the horses and mules. He arrived in Challis February 21, 1879. Next morning saw a dream started, as he strapped on a pair of snow shoes and tramped his way over the mountains toward Custer from Challis, estimating and visualizing the best way, and the cost of making a connecting road.

He left Challis by way of Garden Creek following along the creek bottom until he reached the Klug gulch. There he followed the packtrail up the gulch until he reached the summit. From there he followed the easy grade down the opposite side on the hill fording Mill Creek where Bob Keefer's woodshed now stands. From there he angled up the facing hill zigzagging back and forth until he reached a small lake (now called Slab-Barn Lake). From there he followed the present Pine Summit road, which winds it way again to Mill Creek and on into Custer, a distance of some thirty miles. In one place the original rip-rap can be seen along the side of the road. The old road is still visible by Bob Keefer's.

It was hard to find anyone to make a bid on this road as the old timers were determined it would cost at least $200,000 to build it. By his closest estimation he figured he could have it built at a cost of between $35,000 to $44,000. He finally succeeded in persuading Fred Phillips of Salmon City J.E. Dooley, James Hogle, both of Salt Lake City. W.W. Watkins of Corrine and Fred Myers to each take one fifth and all be partners in this new adventure. It seemed his foresight was always working overtime, because he not only negotiated to build the Custer-Challis road, but at the same time accepted bids to start a stage line from Challis to Blackfoot, which would connect at the railroad. A direct route to Utah. Since he already had many horses, all he had to purchase was coaches and hire drivers for them. He made arrangements to have way stations, feed for the animals and humans. The dream became a reality.

With much satisfaction he took a four-horse stage and started the 156 mile trip from Blackfoot to Challis in June 1879. Now the outside world was brought closer to the mines and gold.

One of the first contracts he undertook was the hauling of the Twenty-stamp mill from Blackfoot to the Custer mines with all the necessary equipment and supplies. He was so sure of his dream, he brought the mill into Challis June 1879 knowing it would be an incentive for the builders to put forth their best efforts. With the Blackfoot line established the Custer road was officially started, also in June of the same year. None of the dire predictions came true. With many men and teams of horses the road progressed with remarkable speed, and was a rough draft when the first wagon bumped its way over it December 24, 1879. It was officially opened and ready for use with a daily line January 1, 1880. At this time the owners purchased a charter from the Idaho Legislature to collect toll. They charged $5.00 for each wagon and team of four animals, and $.50 for each additional span; man on horse back was charged $.50; pack animals were $.25; loose animals other than hogs and sheep were $.25; and sheep were $.10. Practically all the money was spent on keeping the road in repair. It was a long process to recover the money spent on the investment.

Now the link was complete. Leaving Blackfoot and arriving in Challis, the time was just twenty-four hours, which was actually better time than the train on the Utah and Northern Route. The first dinner station from Blackfoot was Big Butte; the next Battleground; and the third about twelve miles from Challis at the foot of the mountain. This route was handled by four drivers, the last man, having the hardest shift, drove his stage into Challis and back again to the foot of the summit.

Immediately mail contracts were negotiated, which was a most welcome addition to the news-starved people of Challis, Custer, and Bonanza.

It took over 150 head of horses to keep the three stage-routes going. (Alex had also taken on another route from Arco to Bellevue.) A great many wagons were also in use to haul feed and supplies for the animals and dinner stations.

Alex negotiated a contract to haul the bullion from the Custer mine. These bars weighed 125 pounds, each worth from $2500 to $3000. They freighted one bullion every day, and on the second day generally hauled two, averaging ten bars a week. Altogether they freighted out $4,500,000, receiving $.14 a pound for taking it to the railroad. One week the snow was so deep it prevented them from hauling anything but the mail; so the packers brought the bullion out by pack-train, down the Salmon River into Bayhorse where it was sent the usual way to the railroad in Blackfoot. There the railroad refused to load it all into one car, so two had to be engaged.

Two and one half years later, Alex was underbid on the lucrative government mail contract, thereby losing his most productive source of revenue. Accordingly, he sold out his share of the stagelines.

With few holdings left in Idaho he moved to Corrine, Utah, a place where a great many of his old freighting and riding companions were living.

Knowing that Alex was a responsible citizen who would "get things done," the townspeople voted him as Mayor, a position he enjoyed.

The time came when he could no longer travel on the stages and the exciting routes of his youth. In 1919 at the age of eighty he wrote a book called "Reminiscence of Alexander Topance." He relates his adventures as a pioneer in Wyoming, Montana, Nevada and Idaho. He recalls his own personal life and says he married Kate Collins, September 18, 1870.

She was born in the Old Fort at Salt Lake, the fourth white child born in Utah. She was widowed when her husband was killed at White Pine, Nevada, leaving her with two boys.

Alex loved his ready-make family. He enjoyed helping bringing them up to be strong men, and spent many evening hours telling them of his own adventuresome, daredevil life.

Ironically this strong man, who had owned ranches, slaughter houses, butcher shops, built roads, ran stagelines, owned mines, bartered, traded, and entertained more schemes and ideas than ten average men, lived out his last few years financially destitute, but rich in a million memories.

Topance road replaced the need for many pack strings.

(Top LtoR) Katie; Alex.
(Bottom) Topance stages ready to depart from Challis.

Wagons on the Topance road from Custer to Challis.

SAMMY HOLMAN "HELLO"

As Sammy sprang down from the seat of the light buggy, he tipped his hat to some lady acquaintances casually waved his footman on, and entered the tall office building with the light grace only small, debonair men seem to have.

He greeted the people in the lobby as he hurried across and ran up the stairs, two at a time with the eagerness of a young boy.

As he turned down the hall, he stopped to unlock his office and backed away, to read again the black letters on the gold plaque, "Samual A. Holman, Attorney-at-Law." Stepping close he used his right sleeve to rub lightly over it, dusting away an imaginary speck.

As he entered his office, Sammy's eyes scanned the desk, furnishings, and rows of law books. Putting his fashionable hat and coat on the coat tree, he settled himself at the desk, pulling yesterday's legal work toward him with good intentions of starting the day's work. Somehow he had trouble; his mind kept playing tricks on him. He thought how lucky he had been from July 24, 1845, here in Saratoga, New York, when he had drawn his first breath in his parent's lavish home. He thought of all the years of school and hours spent with his tutor learning Latin verbs and Greek Philosophy, of parties he had attended, dance lessons, social graces learned, and hours spent in church. Then the years at Cambridge, attending Harvard law school. The climax was when he had taken the bar examination and had received his degree in law.

As his thoughts flipped back, he jumped up from his chair and danced a couple of quick polka steps. He had actually been accepted for marriage by his dark-haired beauty, Kathrine, whom he had been madly courting for the past three months.

He felt he could dash out and tell the world, but his steps slowed as he realized he must now act like a dignified lawyer. Reluctantly he again settled at his desk. However, the legal work suffered for he called on his father at the bank office and informed him he was now interested in the property which he had purchased for him. They discussed architects and the architecture of houses. Then Sam promised to bring his future wife to see the location that afternoon.

Weeks slipped by and it became a ritual for Sammy to leave his office at the end of the day, drive his brougham, drawn by matched bays, to the home of his girl. They would ride to their future home and eagerly scan the buildings, noting the new improvements.

One evening Sammy rang the bell, and waited in vain for the door to be thrown open by Kathrine. Instead he pushed the button time and time again. At last a maid with red, swollen eyes opened the door. As he removed his hat and coat she tearfully told him about his young lady. In the early hours of the morning, Kathrine had been stricken with an acute pain in her right side. After consultation the doctors packed her in ice to alleviate her pain.

Sammy was ushered into Kathrine's bedroom. Her beautiful wavy hair was spread loosely around her flushed face. As he knelt by her side, he noticed her blue unseeing eyes were darkened with reflected pain, and her incoherent speech brought an anguished prayer to spare her life. A nauseous fear gripped him with dread, which seemed to settle into his very being.

Sammy stayed by her side, leaving only to relinquish his chair to her parents and family. The hours slowly ticked away, as the third dawn approached her shallow breathing ceased.

Sammy never entered his law office again. As they lowered his love into her grave, he turned his back on Saratoga. With his lifelong friend Ed Brisbin, he vowed to leave the places where his remembrances were too painful.

His parents helped him pack what possessions he would need. With saddened hearts, they watched as the boys boarded the cars headed for the West.

When the train made the stopover at Rochester, Minn. they decided to stretch their legs and tramped through the town. It seemed to suit them, and Sammy stayed there two years. During this period of time he was appointed Register of the Land Office there.

The ever-present sounds of westbound trains as they chugged and whistled into town, immigrants milling about, more and more young men boarding the cars for the gold fields, led Sammy to throw caution to the winds. He left for the Montana Territory.

There he developed the "Iron Rod" claim and put up an arastra which helped him take care of his discovery of gold and silver. It was here Ed again joined him.

When this claim started to fizzle out, he sold it and left with Ed on the stage for Boise Basin. Sammy again set up an arastra at Silver City. His claim there was not spectacular, but it kept him in enough dust to inhabit the saloons and buy drinks for himself and his friends.

He still had his trunk of tailored suits and hand-turned shoes, but more and more he wore the rough clothes of the miners, course woven pants, and woolen shirts.

Sam was no longer the stable young man who had anticipated a sedate life as a city lawyer. He was eager to answer the restless call of "moving on."

While he walked and listened, he checked out old claims, and looked at likely overcroppings of rock. He was still undecided where to settle. While passing time at a little smoke-filled bar he overheard some conversation which caught his attention. An English company was trying to buy the General Custer mine. Sam had made a thorough study of the terrain in question. His conclusion had been that travel from Bonanza to the Custer mine would be almost impossible, once winter set in. With that idea in mind, he saddled his horse and rode toward the area just below the mine. As he rounded the bend and saw the scarred face of the mountain high on his right, he visualized business buildings and houses scattered on the valley floor. After scouting the area, Sammy, Mardeff and Black laid out the town of Custer. Sammy and Doc Adair threw up the first cabin in 1878.

He built a table in one corner of it where he set his few law books and sketches of the plots of this new town. (Mardeff and Black offered lots free to people who would build on them, but Sammy waited a few weeks, then made a modest profit on his.)

The new town needed legal advice and law, so Sam again found himself involved. He was elected the first Justice of Peace. To quench his thirst for gold-fever, he staked a claim, built the first arastra there and took out the first silver quartz bullion.

Sammy stayed with civilization at Custer for six years. Then in the spring of 1894 he packed up his belongs and rode over the hills to Slate Creek, where he soon located a claim. As he had used up his money and had none for a grubstake, Con Sullivan staked him. This proved to be a wise decision. Clayton Smelting Company bought the claim from them at a price of $27,000 -- equally divided with Con.

After the sale of this property moving was a necessity, so he and "Shorty" Ericson (his partner) located a likely looking mineral spot and staked a claim. This claim was located on a small creek. (It was soon called Holman Creek.) Here he built a cabin which was to be his home for the rest of his life.

Sammy was 49 years old when he made his last move. Because of his habit of stepping to his door and calling, "Hello -- light and come in" to every stranger within earshot, he became known as "Sammy Holman -- Hello".

As the years rolled by the debonair young Saratoga lawyer was no longer visible. In his stead grew a small, grizzled man with haphazard clothing, mended brogans, and scraggly white whiskers.

Nevertheless, the moment of truth was evident when Sam eloquently held forth on legal matters, or world affairs. When the occasion demanded, his fine Spencerian handwriting was a dead giveaway to his earlier beginnings.

With Sammy a pattern had been set. He struggled with day to day existence -- always the gleam of a new strike tomorrow. When the loneliness drove him to seek companionship, he hitched his horse "Old Ten Cents" to his two wheeled cart and he jogged to Clayton. There, he would visit and drink until he slumped unconscious in his chair. When this occurred his friends would load him gently on his cart and Old Ten Cents would take him home sometimes standing patiently by the cabin for hours until Sammy awoke.

He frequently spent evenings with the Con Sullivan family, who rather adopted him. Here he accepted the warm family love which he had missed in his own life. The children adored him. They eagerly watched for his old horse and cart to come bumping down the road. He was also a frequent visitor at the Small Brothers ranch and spent a great deal of time with his partner "Shorty Ericson."

The years marched on and his generous heart had depleted his slender bankroll. More and more he took meals with the Sullivans.

One early spring when all the bridges were washed out and Aileen Sullivan became ill, Mrs. Sullivan desperately needed medicine to help control Aileen's sore throat. Sammy came for a visit. After taking in the situation he volunteered to go to Challis through the mountains and to bring back the supplies she needed.

He traveled steadily through the soft mud and crusted snowbanks. He made good time on the trip in; ate a hasty meal; purchased the medicine; and plodded back over the mountains.

Friends visiting the Sullivan's home remarked,

"Sarah, you sent the wrong volunteer. Sammy will never get past the first saloon."

She replied,

"You only think that you know Sam Holman. When he said that he would help Aileen, he meant it. He will never stop until he either drops in his tracks or he returns with the supplies. He loves these children."

Long after dark, as Sarah sat sponging her child with cool water, changing the cold compresses on her throat, she heard a thump on the porch and then a knock on the door. She opened the door to find a weary Sammy, holding out the bag of medicine.

When his horse died, Sam was forced to catch rides into Clayton with neighbors. One day he went into town with Charlie Small and a friend. As they enjoyed their whiskey and company at the bar time passed swiftly. Sometime in the early morning hours the three men started for home in Charlie's buggy. As they rounded the sharp, narrow turn just below the present Clayton Ranger Station, Charlie pulled the team too close to the road edge, causing the outside horse to lose his footing. Buggy, men and team became a scramble of legs, bodies and moans as they rolled to the bottom of the steep embankment. When Sam tried to free himself from the tangle he felt a sharp pain in his neck. He found that he could not keep his head from falling back on his shoulders.

He was now quite sober. Quietly he told his friends that he was unable to help them with the horses. After questioning Sam, Charlie jumped on one of the horses and rode for help. When the neighbors arrived, they took Sam home and helped him to bed never dreaming that he had a broken neck.

The next morning, he stumbled around until he found a forked stick that was spread enough to slip on either side of his neck. He put a leather belt around his waist, securing the bottom of the stick with another strap under his arms. This kept the stick firmly in place, cradling his neck and allowing his head to remain in an upright position. (He wore this brace day and night for several years.)

During one cold and bitter December night, the wind blew the stovepipe from Sammy's cabin roof. As the room filled with smoke, Sammy jumped from his warm bed and went outside, not taking time to find a coat. Fighting heavy snow, a cold wind and darkness, he managed to find the pipe and to replace it on the roof. He had become thoroughly chilled in the effort. He returned to bed, but it was hours before he could become warm and comfortable.

When Sam did not make his usual appearance at the Sullivan home, Jerry went to check on him. He found the old man in a deplorable condition. He was in the last stages of "the old man's friend" -- pneumonia.

Jerry built up the fire; waited until the fire had become hot; shut the damper and front of the stove; then rode as fast as his horse could go. Jumping from his horse, he flung open the door and shouted, "Our old friend is almost dead! Come and help!" His sister Sadie rushed to her nurses bag, hurriedly put on winter clothes and followed he brother out the door.

His friends were still helping him when Sammy crossed the divide on December 15, 1910. He rallied just before dawn, raised himself on one elbow and softly asked Sadie, "Is the door open?" Then he fell back on his pillow.

After his death the sorrowful Sullivans brought the old man's body to their home. His funeral services were conducted from there.

The gentle little friend, who had somehow helped each one with advice and friendship was sorely missed from his haunts. He lies sleeping far from New York, in the little graveyard at Clayton.

Postscript: Sammy never ceased to mourn his lost love and was heard to quote many times when he was in his cups that "tis better to have loved and lost then never to have loved at all."

As long as Tillie Sullivan Ennis lived, she placed a bunch of wild spring flowers on his grave each spring to remember the hours she had sat at his knees while he whittled wooden dolls for her and talked to her as a friend.

"FROM THE SILVER MESSENGER OF NOVEMBER 2, 1909"

A copy of a letter from Sammy Holman to Edward Brisbin:

Dear Ed:
    I might say I am the "daddy" of Custer county and mining camp of General Custer. I helped to organize it, was its first Justice of the Peace and put up the first quartz mill and arastra, something like I had at Silver City or Iron Rod in Montana when you drove up to my arastra with two yoke of ox and found me grinding out the gold and silver. I took out the first silver quartz bullion or retort ever taken out of Custer county 31 years ago. I discovered the Silver Rule mine, containing lead, gold and silver 25 years ago and sold it to Clayton Smelting Co. They built a wagon road to the mine 20 miles in length. It was afterward merged into the Salmon River road, and if you follow it you will arrive at my place. I have a placer claim which I am not working now for lack of water, a garden, a couple of tons of hay, and plenty of good grass range. I had three old pet horses up to last spring and like your old horse, they would always take me home. Two of them got caught in a snow drift and died; the other, to set me a foot for the first time in twenty-five years had to get the colic and die. If you come up to see me, try to get two plugs of worn out team horses that will stand packing tin cans and pike shovels, and I will make it worth your while to do so.
    I have three fine lead, silver and gold smelting veins or leads with tunnels on the veins with ore in sight; not very large rich paystreaks at present, but every indication of enlarging to pay leads. They run from 20% to 60% less. I cannot work ore with the arastra with over 10% lead as the lead spoils the quicksilver. Come up if you can and inside of two years we will take a last look at Saratoga "in-cog" or any old way. If you conclude not to come, write me and let me know. I see the mail stage coming, so will close I send my likeness.

                Samuel A. Holman

Sammy Holman

The town of Custer that gave Sammy such pride, later had many children and animals. Peek-a-boo the mule was one of the animals that all the kids loved. This picture was taken at the turn of the century: Driver, Grover Curley, the little girl presumed to be Mae Dillen Sullivan.

CALL ME COWBOY JOE

Previous stories have revealed the lives of our Idaho Pioneers, their trials and triumph. No western story was ever complete without the stories of "The fallen Lillies," such as Cowboy Joe. Through research two stories have come to light. Although the stories agree on several points, they are totally different. It seems feasible to publish both versions. Here is the first story.

Hard luck dogged the footsteps of Amanda Friedman all the days of her life. She was born on a farm not far from the town of Council Bluffs, Iowa, in 1854. When she was two years old her parents both died during a severe flu epidemic, leaving her and her two older brothers orphans. The boys were old enough to help out with farm work, so they were given a home by some neighbors. Amanda was placed in a Catholic convent where she knew only the kindly administrations of the nuns. When she was six years old a Catholic family adopted her, and she again had a home. She was loved, taught the gracious manners of a lady, and graduated from a high school in Omaha in 1872, when she was eighteen years old. While doing some shopping she met a young Irish boy who soon came courting her. In less than a year after she met him ,they were married; and he took her home as a bride to Clerinda, Iowa. They were deeply in love and Amanda appreciated the open love and attention of young McLean.

The tales of rich ore strikes and everlasting call of adventure caused them to leave his job, family and friends and to head for the West. Since they started with very little money, they were forced to stop at Ogden, Utah, where he procured a job as grader for the Union Pacific. He worked for the rest of the year, and by spring they had saved enough to take them to Butte in Montana Territory. This town suited their thirst for wild adventure.

All the love and admiration for each other they shared in a tiny house they rented on the outskirts of town. The blow fell when Jim's miner friends brought his shrouded body home.

Probably the only thing that saved Amanda's sanity was the desperate need for a job. She found work in a Norwegian boarding house. There she met Clancy Yates. He had worked with Jim in the mine, but left the mines and had an almost-completed saloon in Bonanza, Idaho. He convinced Amanda that she would enjoy the rugged life and he would pay her well for serving drinks at the "Almira".

She packed her meager belongings and made the backbreaking trip over the rough and narrow, steep trails of the Yankee Fork Country. It was a long, arduous journey in the spring of 1879. The welcome she received at the end of this trip was heartwarming. The miners declared a holiday for the arrival of an honest-to-God, real woman in Bonanza They came from tents, hovels, and cabins to witness the arrival of Amanda. She was no disappointment to them. Her bright auburn hair was worn in the latest style. Her gown was becoming and her large frame was well proportioned. She had a ready smile and a voice that was soft and lady-like. They all fell in love with her winsome ways. Scarcely a day passed that she did not receive a proposal of marriage -- some days, several. The men were lonely and she listened to their troubles. She had great sympathy for them and was a willing audience. She would join in a drink with each suitor as she quietly rejected him. The memory of Jim was still too vivid in her mind. She put in her shift at the "Almira," then she would go her lonely way to her tent-house. The combination of her lost love and the impact of the raw liquor caused the break down of a lovely lady.

   By the end of the first summer, she was often too drunk to make her way home, and would finish out the night with her head across her arms on the poker table. Clancy Yates felt great remorse at her downfall, and tried to persuade her to go back to Iowa where her foster people were. Her only response was to shrug her shoulders and pour another drink. Eventually he was forced to hire one of the new women that had drifted into town. Now Amanda had no means of support, so she used the oldest profession, and went home with anyone who would furnish her with a bottle.

   If anyone asked her about her people she would deny she had any real folks and finally denied her own name. Her upbringing would not allow her to admit her own ruination. When a stranger asked her name, her quarrelsome and testy answer was, "You'll never again hear my name. From now on it's Cowboy Joe, so call me that and leave me alone."

   She drifted all over the gold country and one night was in "Slims" in Sawtooth City in her usual position, passed out with her head on the poker table. Her current friend, Johnny Bee, was playing poker with a miner, Mike Cline. Johnny was down to his last pile of dust and had a hot hand coming. While searching all his pockets, his eyes took in Cowboy Joe, and feeling that he would win anyway offered her as a $50.00 bet. Not to be outdone, Mike accepted the offer and won her. He bought a bottle of whiskey, threw Cowboy Joe over his shoulder and stepped into the night.

   Around noon the next day, Mike sauntered down the trail leading into town. Johnny was watching from the corner of the cabin. When he felt confident that Mike was really on his way to town, he rushed into the cabin and found Cowboy Joe laying on the bed in a stuporous sleep. Since he was a small man and Cowboy Joe was large and unmanageable, he wheeled Mike's wheelbarrow in alongside the bed, and rolled her into it. Her legs and arms gave him trouble, but he tucked them in and wheeled her to his cabin.

Mike had the reputation of being mean and hard-boiled. Johnny was uneasy as he watched Mike's approach later, from a peephole at his window. The roar that came from outside the cabin was ominous and frightening. Johnny stepped out to try to reason with Mike only to receive a bullet within inches of his head, striking a rock behind him. Running sideways, he ducked behind a rock as a series of shots splattered in his tracks. With the gun in hand and shooting whenever Johnny stuck his head out, Mike loaded Joe into the wheelbarrow and wheeled her back again.

With the first shot fired, people all over town poured out of their cabins to witness this hilarious event, and Johnny Bee had a new name -- Johnny-Bee-Hind-the-Rock, a nickname that stayed with him until he left the Yankee Fork Country.

Cowboy Joe went home with anyone who had the price of a bottle. She married a man by the name of Merritt. He must have died, because in one of her sober moments she married Pete Alberts. She lived with him at Old Casto, where he had a claim, but her life was no longer geared to one man. She wondered back and forth from Loon Creek to Custer. She lived in hovels, dugouts, and tents. She had also found the forgetfulness of opium and became a drug addict. The price of opium and alcohol was prohibitive, so she wandered broken, penniless and forsaken to the county poorhouse in Challis.

Amanda's withdrawal was without benefit of a plush establishment, merely accomplished by the lack of funds. She was a heavy tobacco smoker, and Bob Boyd (having the contract for the care of the county poor at the time) furnished her with enough money so she could have a ten cent sack of Bull-Durham occasionally.

Her broken health caused her death. On November 21, 1923 she expired, leaving only an old battered suitcase containing a few outdated clothes, and her one prized possession, a fine gold watch. When the back cover was snapped open, the forever young face of Jim McLean smiled up at you. This treasure she preserved, never forsaking it, even for a fix or a bottle of whiskey.

This was part of Bonanza, one of the towns where Amanda had lived.

THE PRICE WAS A BOTTLE

This is the second version of Cowboy Joe's Life.

Amanda Alberts known to Custer Country as Cowboy Joe, was a Custer County character. She hailed from everywhere and nowhere, and ended in the Custer County poorhouse, with no family, and no friends -- a pitiful lonely figure.

Her early training was evident by her quiet speech, and she was known to boisterously laugh aloud. When she was particularly pleased, she would chuckle. Her acquaintances described her as almost six feet tall, with reddish-brown hair, often worn with two large braids wound around her head. She had bluish-grey eyes and a proud figure. When she first came to Bonanza, she was portrayed as a beautiful woman. Everyone spoke of her as being kindhearted.

When she was in the Yankee Fork country ten years, she had given most ways of living a trial. She was a drifter, and seemed destined to destroy herself.

At one time she stayed with the Arthur McGown family while Arthur went to Ketchum for a load of freight. Arthur had brought her home with him, together with a bottle of whiskey to sober her up. Her attire smelled to high heaven and so did she. Della McGown was a small person and had no clothing that would fit Joe, so she gave her a large pair of Arthur's pants to wear and a shirt. Then they washed all of Joe's clothes. One of her rare chuckles was heard as she glanced down at her pants. When visitors came that afternoon, Joe hid in the bedroom. (No woman was ever known to wear pants in those days). As soon as the wash was dry and ironed, she and Della armed themselves with towels, soap, and clean undergarments, and headed for a nice spring hidden from the public. They had a great time, splashing, soaping, and getting Joe clean. When they returned to the cabin, and Joe was again dressed she was ashamed of her hair and asked Della if she would help her comb it. Della undertook the job. However, Cowboy Joe pleaded to have just one drink so she could stand the pain. It took all day to untangle the matted hair, and while she was having her hair combed, she began to tell Della her life's story. It seemed to take her mind off the hair pulling. She spoke of where she had been before coming to the McGown's. She had been with a fellow staying in an old log cabin with only part of a roof. It was back up in the timber close to the Vienna mine and about five miles from the town of Sawtooth. She didn't know how long she had been with him. But figured about a month. She had been drunk all the time. One morning a howling dog awakened her. She raised her head off a sack of hay (the fellow had stuffed under her head) only to find she was alone with an empty demi-john and the dog. Thinking the dog must be as thirsty as she was, she staggered over and untied him. He headed for water with Joe close behind.

She said, "Us two dogs had a long big drink."

The dog started down the creek on a little path. After looking around, Joe realized she was lost, so she stayed close to the dog, following along until they found a wagon road. They stayed on this until they came into the town of Sawtooth. She went into the saloon to find out where she was. The bartender seemed sorry for the poor half-starved dog, so Joe gave it to him. As the men started to drift into the saloon, they began buying drinks for her. Soon she was drunk and passed out again. This was her condition when Arthur brought her home to Della. She told Della, "My husband, Pete Alberts, always comes and gets me sooner or later; so I will stay here until he comes."

She continued her story and said she was born at Council Bluffs, Iowa. Her mother was a God-fearing, pie-biting Baptist.

When she spoke of her father, her voice took on a tender note as she told of evenings when the work was all done. They would light the lamps. He would take her on his lap, cradling her in his arms and telling her wonderful stories of his childhood.

He died when she was ten years old. After his death her mother put her in a Catholic Sisters' school where she remained until she was sixteen years old. Then her mother came with a new husband and took her home with them. This man was good to Amanda and she was glad to be released from the convent.

One night her mother went to a church meeting and left her, with her stepfather at home. Being lonesome for a father's love she sat down on his lap trying to recapture her childhood. He was rather astonished, but being a kind man, felt he understood her loneliness. He was telling her of his early struggles and how he hated to leave his own mother when he ran away from home. When her mother walked into the room, she misunderstood the situation, grabbed Amanda by the hair and threw her on the floor. She was furious as she turned on her husband who was trying to reason with her. Seeing he could not help Amanda, he walked to the door and disappeared into the night.

Her mother went to a closet and flung a carpet sack at Amanda telling her to pack and leave. As she was packing, she hoped her mother would relent or at least give her some money so she would have something to eat. The only help she received from her mother was a push out the door, as it slammed behind her. Her stepfather was waiting for her and pressed a twenty dollar gold piece into her hand, telling her to go to her mother's minister where she would be sure to have shelter until she could find a permanent place to stay. That was the last time she ever saw her mother or stepfather.

She went to the minister's house. When he heard her he said,

"You must have been very wrong for your lovely mother to put you out, so I cannot help you." She wandered from there to Main Street where the saloons were doing a great business. The windows were all lit up, the music was drifting out of the doorway.

After standing outside of one for a little while, a young man came through the doorway and took something to his horse which was tied at the hitching rack. As his eyes became accustomed to the dark, he made out the figure of this young girl, peering into the bright lights. It was cold where she stood, so he asked her, "Would you like to go indoors where it is warm?" Seeing that she was timid he took her by the arm and lead her in, saying, "I'll take care of you."

This was a different world, music playing, everyone having a good time.

She said,
>"I kept thinking of the cold reception I had received at the two "Houses of God", and of the warm greeting I received at the "Devils Palace."

This young man said his name was Bob, and bought a hot drink for her, which seemed to warm her, and at the same time it helped give the surroundings a rosy glow. By the time she had sampled two more drinks, she felt she had known her companion forever. It was getting late. Turning to her he asked, "Why don't you come home with me? My home is a sheep camp ten miles back in the hills."

They rode all night. Just as the sun was coming up, they arrived at camp. It was in beautiful country. Wherever she looked it was green and had all varieties of wild flowers.

The tent was comfortable, contrasting with the convent and her mother's home. She learned to cook and keep their tent-home in first class shape. She also went with Bob to tend the sheep in the daytime. This episode of her life was a happy one.

About a month later she was standing in the tent doorway when a man drove up in a buckboard. He was hungry, so she prepared a meal for him. Being hospitable, he offered her a drink from a demi-john he brought from the buckboard. It was a generous drink. He told her he was on his way to Utah, to work on a cattle ranch. She thought of that bottle of whiskey, and when he suggested she leave with him, she grabbed her carpet bag and climbed aboard wagon. She left Bob a short note telling him she was leaving for Utah and thanked him for his hospitality.

When they arrived at the ranch, all she knew of her situation was the man's name which was Sam. He bought her a sidesaddle, a riding habit, and a fine mare. She rode the range with him and became and excellent rider. She stayed with him for four years. In fact their plans were made to have the knot tied whenever a preacher came through their country.

One day the boss came by and offered Sam a job as foreman over a new spread he had bought in Wyoming. He accepted the job and left the next morning, leaving money for Amanda to join him in a month.

She was helping round up some steers that were to be driven to the new ranch when she saw a dust-trail in the distance. As it came closer she could make out a well-dressed, man riding a beautiful sorrel mare and leading a packhorse. (Bill later told her, he was pleasantly surprised to find the head-rider was a girl with beautiful red hair. He said he had been impressed with the ease she sat her horse and the way she seemed to be having a great time, herding and pushing the herd.)

Since it was almost chow time she invited him to ride into camp with her. He had a jug tied to his saddle and taking the cork from it he offered he a drink. Bill told her he was tired of life he had been leading and was heading for the gold fields of Idaho. By the time dinner was over, she had decided to leave with him. When he playfully suggested she do so, Joe packed her bag, caught up her horse, and headed for a new adventure.

It took them two weeks to get to Challis, After staying all night, they went over the hill to Custer. There he rented a shack for her, and went to work at the mill, boarding at the boarding house. She was lonely again. With time on her hands, she started to drift into the saloons, soon spending most of her time there.

She said, "Water was scarce, whiskey was plentiful, and the miners were generous with their drinks."

She went on a prolonged drunk. When she sobered up Bill was gone, taking her horse, but leaving her the saddle. She never heard from him again.

She had been friendly with Pete Alberts, and in 1886 she married him, living with him in different places, mainly Casto, on Loon Creek, where he had a cabin and a claim. She lived with him on and off for the next twenty years. She had a habit of getting dry and heading down the trail. For the first few years Pete would follow her and bring her back Eventually he tired of this.

She had also found another release from reality. she had started to shoot morphine. As this habit grew, she was unable to stay on Loon Creek, so she moved to Bonanza.

The last permanent home she had was with Capt. Varney. When he died she wandered into Clayton, a lost soul, heading for Challis and the poorhouse. Someone put her on the stage for the Blackfoot asylum to cure her habit. The asylum released her as cured, but Cowboy Joe remarked, "It is hard to support a habit with no money."

She came back to Beardsley Hot Springs where the poorhouse was located and went on the county.

On November 21, 1923 she was found dead in her room.

The pauper patients were buried in pine boxes. The only box left was two sizes too small for her. The coroner forced Cowboy Joe's body into it and fastened the lid. He failed to tuck in all of her hair.

The lone buggy following the coffin to the grave contained Della McGown. She saw the lock of hair as the breeze caught it. It seemed to her that Cowboy Joe was waving goodbye.

Amanda

CUSTER'S FIRST LADY

ClaraBelle Washington Riley Thompson was born February 22, (thence the middle name of Washington) 1858 at St. Louis, Missouri. Her parents, Allen and Sarah Riley came from Carlisle, Cumberland, England and settled first in the frontier town of St. Louis where Allen plied his profession of of upholsterer.

They resettled in Omaha, Nebraska. It was from there Allen volunteered his services for his new country, and served as a Captain in the Union Army.

When he returned to Omaha he found it to be a poor town for an upholstery and furniture business. All available men of the town had spent time in the army, leaving hundreds of families who had been living on army pay. Therefore Allen, his wife and growing family of four children, traveled to the thriving city of Salt Lake City, November 15, 1859, riding on the first Union Pacific train.

Here Allen felt he could succeed in his profession and his children could have the advantages of good schools. (When the family was complete it consisted of five girls, Laura, Lizzie, Belle, Sallie, and Annie, and two boys, Julian and Allen.)

In those days great emphasis was placed on manners, social graces, and education. The Rileys not only had these standards to live by, but their mother's strict English standards as well. They were expected to and did, bring home high marks from school. In their free time at home the boys apprenticed under their father, learning the furniture and upholstery trade; and their mother schooled the girls in needlecraft, cooking, budgeting and managing a home. Each child was encouraged to develop his talents. Belle chose the millinery trade, apprenticing under one of the best milliners in Salt Lake. It was a thriving business as all well-dressed ladies wore hats whenever they were in public. Belle fashioned hats for her family plus selling them to friends and acquaintances.

It was the custom of our country at that time for young girls of seventeen and older to receive calls at home from young men. The home at 228 East 4th South, where the Rileys lived followed this rule. All five girls had young men calling, escorting them to church, young people's church groups, operas, masquerades, balls, teas, and musical affairs.

All five were tiny women (Belle was 4'10" wore size 4 shoe and weighed no more than 95 pounds for many years.) They were all dressed in the height of fashion; able to do this by selective choosing of the best materials, thriftly fashioning them, and taking meticulous care of the garments.

Most families encouraged their girls to marry men who were established with a trade or business which would enable them to provide for a wife and family. Consequently women had a tendency to marry older men.

Belle had been escorted about town by several young men and was receiving numerous letters every week from would-be suitors. She was still flirting with a carefree heart, until one day Sallie brought her escort and his friend home for afternoon tea.

George Bordman Thompson was not the same man when he left the Riley home as he had been when he walked into the warm, friendly house. His attention was caught by the auburn haired girl, whose stylish hairdo included a curl tucked becomingly to one side. Her charming English manners and winsome ways soon had him completely captivated. He began calling regularly several evenings a week.

George was a man forty-two years old. At the time of his first acquaintance with Belle, he was owner of several mining interests and was also using his education as a geological engineer.

Belle was soon comparing George's polished manner and air of command with the callow awkward youths who seemed always at her elbow.

During the many evening while Belle and George were visiting he explained why he had left his settled life in Maine to start a new one in the West. He told of growing up in a large family where education was placed above everything but God. His family made many sacrifices for this cause. George had received honors in engineering and school teaching. His brothers were lawyers, ministers, and teachers. At the age of thirty he married his childhood sweetheart. They were happily expecting their first child when he lost both his wife and baby during childbirth. At the close of school he sold everything and crossed the Rockies, never to return.

When a suitable time had elapsed, George asked Belle to be his life partner. They were married the second day of April, 1877 in an impressive Episcopal ceremony, conducted by Bishop Tuttle. The reception which followed included half the families of Salt Lake City. (As long as Bishop was able to tour the Western Territories of his Diocese, he always included Custer and Challis in his tour and visited his "Young Lady Belle" as he called her.)

The surrey was at the curb, ready to take the newlyweds into their new life. Piled high on top was Belle's new trunks, containing all the pretty party and practical dresses and coats, the new hats and tiny buttoned shoes of her trousseau which had been carefully sewn, selected and packed. It also contained small items and a few family heirlooms.

The entire family followed them to the surrey, laughing, crying admonishing and cajoling. All the voices mingled at once, wishing them God-speed. The last to bid farewell to Belle was Sarah and Allen. Sarah gave her thin young shoulders a gentle pat and lovingly held her in a final embrace, somehow sensing this daughter was destined for many adventures.

Their honeymoon was spent at Lewiston, Utah, and Tonopah, Nevada, where George owned and managed mines.

George proved to be a gentle husband whose main concern was the welfare of his wife, but he was also a respected man in the world. Gravely concerned with the well-being of the country, he took his civic duties in solemn trust, believing in electing men whose capabilities would further the growth of our country.

George had been hearing the tales of towns in Idaho where the rich gold mines were beginning to ship great quantities of ore to Utah to be smelted. His interest in mining was aroused. He and Belle discussed the possibilities of a move to these mines. He explained the many hardships that would be in such a move and tried to tell of the loneliness which would often befall her. She had great misgivings but had also been reared in a family who believed "whither thou goest, I will go," so she bravely gave her consent to make this move. George began selling all his holdings in both Utah and Nevada and completed all transactions by the spring of 1878.

As July approached and Belle was nearing confinement for her child, George wanted the best doctor available, so they journeyed back to Salt Lake to her parent's home. There their first born son, George Jr., made his appearance July 29, 1878 -- a healthy baby.

After their son was born, George began his preparations for the move to Idaho. He made arrangements with Belle's parents for his wife and child to live with them. He purchased a heavy-duty sawmill, together with a planer and attachments and had them shipped to Challis to await his arrival. He bought windows sashes, doors and molding for their future home and laid in a large supply of food. He bought a heavy duty wagon with horses, harnesses and carpenter tools, nails and packsaddles

When the baby George was one year old, George kissed his wife and child goodbye and left by way of Corrine, Utah, driving one wagon, and leading two saddle horses, while Belle's brother Allen drove another. When they arrived in Challis, they found a storage for their wagons, placed the pack saddles on their work horses, saddled up and rode to Custer. Upon arrival, they set up camp. George immediately found a man by the name of Sammy Holman who had some lots for sale and purchased two from him. They took their string of pack horses and brought in the sawmill that was stored in Challis. It was set up with all possible speed. The first lumber the mill produced was used to make the Thompsons a little two room cabin.

Mail was fairly regular because of the ore pack trains; so Belle was kept informed of progress in Custer. George's letters described the activity of the town. Some were still camping in tents with no preparation for the coming bitter weather, some arrived daily with only the clothes on their backs. He said he was satisfied with his job as the first engineer in the mill.

Her answering letters warmed his lonely heart. She told how their baby was growing and of the fancy work and rugs she was making to brighten their new home.

At long last in June 1879 he wrote her a letter declaring the cabin was finished, and he would meet her train with a wagon at Eagle Rock. Her journal best describes that journey. It gives a glimpse of her life:

"Started for Custer June 20, 1879. We went on the train to Eagle Rock, there Mr. Thompson met me. We traveled from Eagle Rock in a white covered spring wagon (Eagle Rock is now called Idaho Falls, a thriving town and one of the largest business towns in Idaho). At the time I reached Eagle Rock it was just a small railroad stopping place and the end of the line. We traveled the rest of the way to Custer in our covered spring wagon. When we arrived at Battleground on the Lost River I was so nervous, I could not sleep that night, but Mr. Thompson said, "There is no danger of Indians now." When we arrived at Challis, we drove over to VanCamps for a short time, as Mr. Thompson knew them in Utah. Then we continued on our journey to Custer. We passed the ranch we live on now and up over the hill to the tollgate. There we stopped overnight. Then on to where they were making the road. One place we had to take the team off the wagon and lead them around the mountain down to where the road was finished. The workmen took ropes and tied around the wagon and let it down onto the road.

My brother Allen Riley built a two-room log house for us in Custer on the hillside. They had the sawmill at the lower end of Main Street. They shipped in windows, sashes, doors and molding.

We had some very fine gatherings in Custer. We ladies gave dinner and card parties. It was like one big family. The men after the mill was finished, had a big bath-pool. They would bathe, dress up and come down town. You would think they lived in a big city!

I was in Custer 7 months before I saw another white woman. Then one day I looked out on the street, and there in the door of a cabin across the street stood Mrs. Pete Johnson. I called Mr. Thompson and said,

'Oh! George there is a woman. Go bring her over.' He did and we looked at each other and cried for joy. Mrs. Johnson had come off the Custer hill. She was so nice and had a little girl named Katey. George and she played together all the time. Then one day Katey fell into Yankee Fork and George caught hold of her dress and held her till her mother came. Mrs. Johnson said that when she grows up she belongs to George. This was not to be, for Katey died when she was eleven years old -- a victim of pioneer life."

The first year in Custer was a traumatic experience for Belle. She had been reared in a home where there was lots of excitement and girl-companionship, with many of the necessities of life taken for granted. She was plunged in to the raw existence of bare necessities and was alone six days a week, eight to ten hours a day with only the companionship of her baby. Even to see the town the snow had to be shoveled from the windows.

She gradually made the necessary adjustments; women were arriving daily. It was no longer a town of men.

The ladies soon organized picnics, Bible classes, card and dance parties, hosted speakers and itinerant preachers. (The first Easter service was held in a saloon whose gaming tables and other adornments were draped for the occasion.) They entertained in their homes, and also gave freely of their time and helped when illness struck.

By September 1, 1880 Custer was endowed with a doctor; so Belle's second confinement was attended by a capable physician. Little Julian was born in their comfortable homey cabin. When the baby was three months old he began to show stress and pain, whenever he was fed. Then as these symptoms became more pronounced, he began to have convulsions, quite frequently after his feeding. His frightened young mother would plunge him in warm water, which seemed to relieve him immediately. She soon developed a habit of always having a tea kettle of hot water on the stove.

As a popular young matron, Belle, frequently entertained a lady friend or two for lunch. On this day, April 18, 1881, they had just completed a luncheon when Julian began to whimper. Belle's guest suggested that Belle tend her baby while she tided up the kitchen.

Belle fed and cared for him and then as he became drowsy she gently laid him down. While she was drawing a coverlet over him he began to have a seizure.

She grasped him from the bed and rushed for a pan of hot water, only to find the kettle empty -- her friend had just rinsed the dishes. In desperation, Belle handed Julian to her, ran blindly out of the door, stumbling along the walk with heavy skirts held aside, and plunged down the stairs, the empty tea kettle dangling in her hand. As she burst into the McGown saloon, her pale anguished face told the story. George McGown swooped his own kettle from the stove with one hand and reached for Belle's with the other, almost dragging her along with his huge strides. After reaching the cabin Belle clutched her baby tightly, while Mr. McGown poured boiling water into a pan, hastily cooling it. Too late --The baby quivered one last time and was still.

Julian Riley Thompson, age seven months, 18 days was buried in the new graveyard at the edge of town just beyond the mill. The sorrowing community turned out to mourn with them.

George and Belle took up their life again, quietly hiding their sorrow. (Until Belle's own death she made annual pilgrimages to the cemetery every year to decorate and maintain her baby's grave.)

Two more children were born to them, Ethel Belle, and Elizabeth Francis.

Custer was again without a doctor when it was nearly time for Ethel's birth; so Belle made the long journey to Salt Lake City, staying at her parent's home and returning with Ethel when she was two months old. When Lizzie was born, Custer had two doctors.

Custer gradually had taken on a new look. With several sawmills working full time, they had taken their toll of the beautiful trees which had previously given it a look of cabins and tents huddled in forest. There were many large establishment in town with boardwalks running parallel. To them the Nevada House was a glorious affair, and it boasted beautiful rugs, large rooms, lace curtains at the windows, and scrolled woodwork. The town had several saloons, a barber shop, Wells Fargo station, a brewery, and a newspaper. Close to the creek, huddled behind McKensies' livery stable were three prostitution houses -- called the red-light district. They were identified by the red window shades which, when pulled at night with a lamp lit in the room, gave off a red light. Thompsons' contribution to Main Street was the Thompson building. It was two-story building, the lower floor was a furniture store, while the upper section contained seven rental rooms for men. It was directly in front of their home. Since the home was on a hillside, George had constructed a thirty foot walkway directly into the second level, from their front porch, enabling them to have easy access to the rooms, which had to be cleaned daily. It also provided the Thompson family with a way onto the Main Street without shoveling so much snow.

(Years later, after it was leased to others, the Thompson building was used for most of the dances, funerals and large gatherings. It was even reputed to have housed the red-light ladies for a time.)

The ever-present clank and groaning of the mill machinery, with the penetrating whistle which blew for all shift changes and for emergencies, was an accepted noise.

The one great fear which prevailed in all the home and shops was snowslide weather. (For the seven years that Belle lived there during this type weather she would hurriedly do her housework, then sit in one designated spot (as did all the ladies) with her children around her, reading to them, so that if a snow slide came the men would know where to dig.

By the time Georgie was six years old, Custer was a thriving community and needed a school, for which many families at Bonanza and Custer pooled their resources. The first school was held out in the open between Custer and Bonanza using homemade tables and benches. One father put up a tall swing for the children. They attended school there as long as the weather permitted. Meanwhile the concerned citizens were completing a cabin for them.

For sometime George had known his health was failing. His concern grew daily as he considered the future of his young wife and children. He finally decided to buy a ranch where they would be able to make their own livelihood. Thus, he did. The family moved from Custer in the spring of 1886, to the ranch that was located on Garden Creek, just one and one half miles from town. (This ranch is still in business and is known now as the Ray Keppner ranch.)

Their first night in the new home was not as they had anticipated. It was dark by the time they had unloaded and temporarily set up housekeeping.

The new horsehair mattresses, which Belle's father had just shipped to them, were placed on the floor, making up beds for the night. It had been a long and tiring journey over the hill, so every one retired early. As they blew out the light and prepared for sleep they all felt an itching sensation. When the light was relit, behold, the entire house was literally walking with bed bugs. An old "Batch" had lived in the house for years (evidently the bugs hadn't bothered him.) They spent the rest of the night catching as many of the bedbugs as they could and dropping them down the chimney of the lamp. Next morning all their clothes, beds,and bedding had to be removed from the house and fumigated, They camped out in the yard until they had completed this chore.

The Thompsons bought plows, harrows, necessary farm machinery, milk and range cows, work and saddle horses. They planted a large garden and make fences and ditches.

In August when their garden was producing they made trips into Custer with their excess produce. Belle had made butter from cream she had skimmed from long pans of milk, which had cooled in their new milkhouse. She put the butter down in small tubs. These were packed the night before into the wagon which had been lined with green dampened alfalfa hay. The vegetables and rhubarb were packed around them, then more green damp alfalfa was packed on top, for a layer of insulation.

They would leave Challis at night, arriving in Custer just as the sun was coming up. People would come from all over town with pans and containers to buy the firm, sweet butter and the fresh vegetables.

When Ethel was 13 years old, she heard her father utter a strange sound one morning when he was washing up for breakfast. Then he staggered backwards, falling into her arms. He had suffered a stroke.

This sorrowing family nursed and cared for him, but his ailing body gave up the struggle six weeks later, leaving Belle a widow at the age of 38. Lizzie was nine. On George Jr.'s 17 year old shoulders fell the task of being the man of the family. (He had aspired to being a pharmacist, but quietly settled into being a rancher.)

Belle lived to be 86 years old, succumbing on her birthday. She had lived up to her parents' expectations. She had carried her share of marriage, had been one of three ladies who founded the Community Church, had taught Sunday School for many years and was a active member of the Rebekah Lodge.

She proudly welcomed her daughters new husbands into the family, and all the grandchildren and great-grandchildren loved their pioneer grandmother.

Forty-eight years from the time Belle bade George farewell, she was laid to rest by his side.

This petite Salt Lake City socialite who had danced and flirted her way into marriage, captured a man who loved and cherished her and was a guiding light to her three children, had left a community who had benefited by her influence, guidance and counseling.

Her task was complete.

The tall structure on the left with the light roof is the Thompson building. Directly in back is the Thompson house.

(Top LtoR) Belle; George.
(Bottom) Belle and daughter seated on rocks at a Custer picnic.

(Top) George, one of the boys in swing at the first school held between Custer and Bonanza. (Bottom) The Thompson house at Challis ranch: standing, George; seated, Lizzie; Belle with grandson David Philps.

THE STURDY OAK

Life for Ethel Belle Thompson began in Salt Lake City because there was no doctor in Custer City, where her parents made their home. Otherwise she would have had her beginnings in a raw bustling mining town: a fitting place for a person who had a goldmine of inner strength.

She led the usual life of a child in a mining town and was well loved by her family and doting mining friends, many of whom had left behind their own little girls. She had fond memories of playing with friends and attending most social functions with her parents, recalling how she loved to perch on the bed watching her pretty mother as she happily prepared for parties and dances. Ethel loved to touch the shiny satin dresses trimmed in velvet that her mother often wore, and watched closely as Belle swept her hair high on her head, leaving only a curl or two to swing free. After her mother was ready, it was Ethel's turn to be splendidly dressed. Her mother had special party dresses for her, too, with wide bright sashes of red and blue.

When everyone was ready, her parents would take each child by the hand and they would go to the parties, or dances, for babysitters were unheard of. The children would stay awake until their bedtime, at which time they would lie down in places prepared for them.

When it was time for Georgie to go to school, Ethel hated to see him leave her behind. He would pick up his hat and coat each morning, kiss his little sister and mother, then happily swinging his lunch-pail, was off to school leaving behind a very rebellious little girl.

In October, 1886, a strange man came to their home one night and Ethel was sent to spend the night with the neighbors. Next morning her father brought her home. As he set her down on the floor she heard a small mewing sound coming from the corner of the room where her mother was lying in bed. Her father picked Ethel up and held her so she could see into the small bundle on her mother's arm -- her new baby sister, Elizabeth.

The rest of the winter she no longer minded when Georgie trotted off to school. She was allowed to help her mother bathe the baby, and once in a while she was allowed to sit in a chair and hold her.

There began to be an unsettled feeling in the air which even a little girl was able to sense. There was talk of the Thompsons leaving their home and moving to Challis. As a little girl, Ethel wondered how she would like living away from her familiar home and friends.

The day came when the cabin was emptied, and the household goods were piled high on a dead-ax wagon with hardwood bows and a canvas top partly folded back. All the neighbors came to put their arms around her mother and shake hands with her father. Her miner friends swung her high off the ground in a wide circle the way they always had and the way she loved. But this time she felt a wetness against her cheek when they squeezed her tightly against them for a minute before putting her down.

At last the hand-shaking and embracing was over and the wagon wheels start to roll. Seated in front was George Sr. and Belle with baby Elizabeth in her mother's arms. In the back Ethel and George had a snug little spot nestled in amongst the bedding and household articles. They waved to the people until they rounded the bend at the edge of town.

At noon they stopped at the tollgate where they ate their lunch while visiting with the Keene and their girls. After the horses had again been hitched to the wagons, they made the rest of the trip arriving in the late evening at the ranch. As they drove down the lane of their new home, they were a weary but happy family.

Everyone but the baby helped unpack enough to see them through the night. Scouting around Georgie had discovered a row of multiplier onions. Since the Thompson family had never been able to grow a garden in Custer, they no longer wondered what to have for supper. Ethel's mother unpacked the freshly made bread and they made their meal of bread and the onions, with some dried fruit for dessert.

(Excerpts from Ethel's journal) After we were settled the June rains started then we soon found the shed-kitchen leaked like a sieve. Grandpa Riley had been corresponding with Mama and Papa, so he agreed to come visit and do some badly needed carpentry work. They tore off the old shed and added a new kitchen. There were two nice large well-constructed buildings on the ranch, so they hitched up horses, put drags under the buildings and added them to the house. This gave us a large parlor and extra bedroom (later George dismantled a building in Custer reassembled it against our house and added another bedroom. This completed our eight room house.

It was a whole new world to be children. Up to this point we had never had any animals of our own, nor had we lived where we could raise a garden. We had several clucking hens with baby chicks on the place and soon had saddle-horses and milk cows. (From the time I was nine and George was thirteen, we milked 13 cows night and morning; cleaned the barn; put in clean bedding; and tossed down the hay for night. (Papa's fingers had become too crippled to help us.) Sam Tripp, papa's ex-fireman at the mill, prospected in the summers and boarded with us in the winter. He never charged him board, but he helped us all the time and cut green wood, split it and piled it to dry for the coming year. We always had a nice pile of wood. We had a bunch of ranch cattle, but in those days there was no such a thing as white-faces. They were mostly roans, reds, and whites.

In the fall of the year we would pick bushels and bushels of crab apples in our orchard. Using an apple press, we made our own vinegar. We always made at least forty gallons. The first week we dipped into the sweet cider pretty frequently. Next it would go to the tingley stage. Then Mama would say "no more". By this time we generally still had twenty five gallons -- our years supply of vinegar, generously shared with the neighbors.

When we moved on the ranch there was an old Champion mower, a rake and a plow, all very ancient; but we "made do" with them for years.

Each fall when we sold the cattle, we laid in our winter's supplies. The coffee came in large gunny sacks, and our house would smell like coffee for days, as Mama would roast so many pans of the green beans each night, until she had them all baked to the right color.

We bought dried prunes, apricots, peaches, and pears, which were packed in wood boxes. The raisins did not come in sacks as they do now but were pressed into a woodbox still on dried stems. Cinnamon and nutmeg had to be grated.

Communication in Round Valley was by word of mouth; no telephone was installed in the Thompson home until after Ethel was married and left home. The weekly newspaper furnished the national news as well as the local, while the post office bulletin board was eagerly scanned for items of news. Posters of events were placed in all the meeting places. Odd Fellow and Rebekah lodges were gatherings for neighbors to visit as well as lodge affiliation. The school events were eagerly awaited. Spelling bees and orations were highly competitive events. The Thompson children walked a mile each way to and from school all their years of schooling, bringing home the mail with them each night. On Saturday and in summer someone skipped along to get the mail.

A lot of social life evolved around church which was attended each Sunday unless someone was ill. Winter and summer alike saw Ethel, Lizzie and George at the young people's Christian Endeavor.

All the dresses and coats Ethel and Lizzie wore were made by their mother. Many yards of material was included in each dress with tiny stitches, button and tucks for trim. (Many of their coats were made from coats their aunts had sent from Salt Lake. Their mother would carefully rip out the seams; wash and press the wool; then use the inside of the material, which was just like new and fashioned stylish coats for them. (Excerpt):

"I never attended formal school until I was nine years old. The winters were so bitter my father set my lessons for me. When I was nine we attended the school that was located by the graveyard. In winter the stream that flowed by the school would ice up and overflow its banks, creating a wonderful place to skate at noon after we had eaten our lunch. Our school generally started September 15, and ended around May 15.

We packed our lunches in 5 pound lard pails that made excellent lunch containers. Our lunches were generally made with homemade bread, roast beef, pork or ham. Apples from our trees with a piece of pie or cake for dessert.

Because our folks felt children should learn also by experience, each child had so many chores which were listed on a slate board by the door. As each chore was performed, we checked them. When all chores were completed we were free to roam for the day. We spent hours perched on the farm fence which bordered the road watching the pack trains. (Some of the trains would have as many as 81 mules. The favorite place of the packers to stop for the night was just outside our gate, where there was a level place with a small stream of water for animals and camp water. It would take the packers all day to load for the coming trip into Custer, so it would be evening before they could camp. Sometimes two or three men would be required to load the heavy machinery. It always pleased us children to watch the mules as they were unhobbled, go to their own pack-saddles, and to lay down so the men could load them.

Fourth of Julys were something we looked forward to. Everyone seemed to take part in the celebration for our independence. We had picnics and races; sometimes above the old Klug ranch on Garden Creek or sometimes by the old brewery. The old soldiers would send off anvils, putting one on top of the other with powder in between. It would make an awful racket. Dick Hull, the old postmaster, was one of those old soldiers.

After the picnics, the noisy anvils and races, the dance would start. The little babies and smaller children were bedded down on a pile of coats or on some blankets. At midnight there would be a big supper at one of the hotels, then almost everyone went back to dancing until daylight.

I believe the happier time of my childhood was in the evenings after the chores were done.

The woodstoves would be popping and cracking. The lamps gave off a warm glow. And Mama would be settled in her chair gently rocking with some sewing in her hands. We children would pore over our lessons, completing them as quickly as possible because Papa always read a part of a story to us each night. He was a wonderful reader, speaking every word clearly. When it neared bedtime, he would select a very exciting place in the story and lay his book down saying, 'It's bedtime.' Needless to say we always looked forward to the next night's story.

Gradually my father became more crippled. I remember at times seeing him coming from the pasture where he had been irrigating, leaning on a forked stick under one arm and using the shovel under the other arm to get back to the house.

After my father died, our life changed. (Since he had been brought up on a farm and had had to care for the soil and animals, this knowledge was passed on to us before he left us. Mama was a good manager; still, we missed our father's final outdoor decisions."

The neighbors kept an eye on the Thompson family; admired the way young George managed; but if they needed help during threshing, branding or butchering, friends turned up to help them.

"George had always said he was going to be a pharmacist. Eventually I decided that was what I wanted to be too. After Papa died, we both knew this was never to be. However, the winter following Papa's death, Grandpa Riley came to stay, so George could go to Salt Lake City to school for a year. (It's a wonder Grandpa and I didn't starve the cattle to death. He was a city man and I was so young. I would pitch the hay down until we decided it was enough for the day. The cattle came out looking slick in the Spring with nice strong calves at their sides, so I guess we did all right.)

The next Fall was my turn to go to the city. My mother eventually managed for all three of us to have a year in Salt Lake. She cautioned me just before I left, 'Ethel, for this one year, you are to not worry about expenses, or about home. We have amply provided for you to have one year, such as I knew when I was growing up. Your grandmother will see to it, that you do 'so.'

> It was a wonderful year, and I did enjoy the different school and all the sights to see. Still I had been raised so much different than my mother and was contented to go back to my little valley when my year was up.
>
> I submitted to a teacher's examination when I returned home and had secured the teaching position in the Challis Creek School, meaning to report for it that fall. However, at church one Sunday, I met a stranger, who changed my plans completely."

Young men were beginning to tie their saddle horses at the hitching rack in front of the Thompson home. Lizzie had learned to play the organ and many evenings and Sundays the girls and their girlfriends entertained the boys in the parlor gathered around the organ, singing songs while some played an instrument in accompaniment.

As Ethel stepped into the church on a Sunday in March 1901 she noticed a dark-haired nice looking young man -- a stranger. At the end of the service she was introduced to Robert Philps, who was the new dentist. He lost no time making her acquaintance, and was soon visiting at the Thompson home as often as his work would allow.

They were soon in love and two months from the time of their first acquaintance, they were married at her home by Rev. Guy Foster, May 13, 1901.

After the beautiful wedding and hearty congratulations, the newlyweds opened the gifts and placed them on display. Then Ethel's mother and Julia Funkhouser spread a delicious repast of ham sandwiches with salad, cake and coffee for the guests.

From her journal,

> "We spent the first two nights at my home. The first night it was very late by the time all of our friends had wished us well, partaken of lunch and visited with other -- friends they had not seen for sometime. The next day we spent carefully itemizing the gifts and gently packing and storing them for use when we came back to the little house Rob had purchased for us. We had a wonderful time with Mama, Lizzie, and George that day. I also took Rob all over the ranch, sharing with him my girlhood haunts, the forts we children had built and our favorite trees we had climbed. I was secretly saying goodbye to the childhood I was leaving behind.
>
> Next morning Rob and George hitched up the surrey and pulled it in front of the house. We had a grand time, loading it up, deciding what and where to stash things. At last we were ready to go. I had been so

eager to begin this trip that my feet had scarcely touched the ground, but as Rob helped me up into the seat and I glanced down into the upturned faces of my sister and brother, and my tiny mother, I realized I would no longer be skipping up the road to town or school, and would no longer be an intimate part of the family. I had to quickly turn my face to keep from having them see the unexpected tears, which were threatening to fall. I waved goodbye all the way up the lane; but as we turned onto the road, my spirits rose.

As I turned to explain to Rob, he nodded his head and gave my shoulder a pat and then a quick hug.

We were on our way up the river an ideal honeymoon, Rob had dreamed up for us. We were to spend the whole summer traveling from mining camp to camp, working and playing.

Our first stop was about half way to Clayton. We received word that a man there had an abscessed tooth. As we forded the river I was surprised at the big boulders we worked our way around. We spent the night there. They served us a lovely dinner, the first time I had ever seen cornstarch pudding served with a dollop of jelly on top and appetizingly swimming in cream.

The next morning bright and early we left for Clayton. The next two weeks was one of the happier times of my life. We rented a room from Mrs. Dow where we ate and slept. It was located on the river side of the street and Rob rented a room in the Smith's hotel directly across from our room for his office. There I helped him with polishing dental plates and various other tasks. At night we walked up to the Sullivan Hot Springs. We would go swimming first then we would stroll over to the Sullivan's house. I never saw such a family. They had such musical talent, and they would play and sing at the drop of a hat. They were wildly excited about everything. Rob would accompany the girls on the fiddle with such tunes as 'In The Shade of The Old Apple Tree', or 'Redwing'. When it came time to leave we would pry ourselves away and with music and laughter still ringing in our ears, we would walk back to Clayton, holding hands and sometimes dancing a few steps as we walked along. It would be around midnight when we arrived at our room.

Our next stop was Charlie Small's (known now as Saturday Mountain). We had an office in the house and stayed there two weeks. As usual we worked on teeth and dentures in the daytime, but the evenings we continued walking and sometimes we went fishing. We caught fine trout which the Smiths served crisp and brown for breakfast in the mornings.

Next we went to Robinson Bar. It was a stage station where the stage changed horses. Here we again stayed two weeks. We stayed in the hotel there, owned by K. D. Williams. Here for an added entertainment Rob taught me how to swim in a bathing pool there which was naturally hot water. I had never had a chance to learn to swim because although our family enjoyed going to the Challis Beardsley Hot Springs, it was quite an undertaking to hitch up teams and drive there and back: so it was a rare treat when we made an effort. Therefore, to go swimming every night with my husband to teach me was very enjoyable.

When we left each place, I would hate to leave, because we were making new friends and renewing old friendships, and we were having such fun. Our team trotted right along as we took to the road; and as soon as we were on our way, I would look forward to our next adventure.

In this case it was Custer. I could vividly recall our trip out of there when we left it to move to Challis as a small child, and the trips back in when I could accompany my father and brother, bringing produce to sell. This was entirely different. I was coming back to my childhood town on my honeymoon.

We stayed at Burtons; it wasn't exactly a hotel but served meals. We kept our team in the McKensie's livery barn.

We resided there the rest of the summer until October with the exception of seven days up at the Lucky Boy Mine. It took quite a bit to live because of boarding out and also boarding our horses. We still made quite a bit of money for those days

We had a front room rented for the dental office which faced the Main Street with a large front bay window; and we had a bedroom. These were located right next to Arthur McGowns.

The rates Rob charged for dental work were as follows: All plates upper and lower and pulled teeth $25.00; fillings were all the way from $5 to $10; mal gum was $1.75; cement was $1.00, scaled and cleaned $2.00.

Back of the Dunn Hotel was a trail straight up to

the Lucky Boy mine, about one mile long. By road it was at least six miles. On Saturday nights you could hear the men laughing and talking. Some would be singing long before you could see them swing into view with long strides. Some of the men boarded in Custer, so they could come down every night.

> Finally when we were caught up on some of the dental work, we decided to go up to the Lucky Boy Mine. There we stayed 7 days and boarded with my girlhood friend Mable Hellman and her husband Adam. They lived in a rather large two room cabin which doubled for a small boarding house. They insisted on giving up their bed and they slept on the floor. Oh! what a visit we had! While I helped her with her meals, we talked of all the things that had been happening in Challis since she had left. How great it was to share her life again."

With the feel of fall in the air the newlyweds were anxious to return to Challis. They had one last stop at Bayhorse, where they stayed one week, then with all of the work completed, they headed for Challis.

> "It was great fun moving into the little house. (It is the white house directly behind the Challis Drug Store. Then it sat in the middle of the lot where the drug store now stands). Rob had his office on the right front room while the left one was his laboratory."

Those were happy days. After the long struggle of putting himself through school, it was rather nice to watch the bank account grow. The last large expense had been the red velvet dental chair, footdrill and office furniture.

As young marrieds they attended parties, church socials, and lodges. That year Ethel had time to take painting lessons from the minister's wife who was an accomplished artist.

May 4, 1902 David Allen Philps was born to them. Later they became the parents of five other children: Laura, Anabell, Ethel, & Roberta (Robert Thompson Philps died in infancy).

They left Challis when their first child was a baby. Rob felt he needed more education, so they went to Denver, where he received a degree of Doctor of Dental Surgery.

From Denver they went to Idaho Falls, where they lived and prospered for seven years. They were finding life in the city confining, so they came back to Round Valley and bought the 640 acre ranch known as the old Challis ranch. Later they purchased several other ranches in order to supply enough feed for the sheep and cattle they raised. They built a large two-story nine room log house for their home.

They enjoyed working for their success, and Rob continued to be a dentist until one day a deer-fly carrying the tuleremit germ bit him. It affected his nervous system causing his hands to tremble and making it impossible to continue his dentistry.

So he rode the fields he loved and supervised the ranch work.

Ethel and Rob spent a wonderful life together. Their children witnessed a love that lasted; in which trust was the main ingredient. Their positive outlook was an inspiration to their children.

After Rob and Ethel had celebrated their fiftieth wedding on May 13, 1951, Rob became ill and was taken to Idaho Falls to the hospital. There he left his "Sturdy Oak" to carry on alone.

She picked up the reins he had tossed her and continued to successfully supervise the ranching enterprise until June 18, 1975 when she left this part of her life, as quietly as she had lived. Her tired heart quit beating.

Although Ethel had set aside her aspirations to be a pharmacist and she had a natural bent for painting, she had turned her hands to being a help-mate to Rob and to the rearing of her family. The world may have lost a meticulous pharmacist or a budding artist, but the family gained a loving, warm, understanding wife and mother. Her tasks were never so long or hard, that she hadn't time to give comfort.

Truly such a life could have been written in song. From the time she was a baby of a gold camp, to the black-haired girl trudging to school -- a young lady seated daintily at a church picnic, and a sparkling-eyed young woman in love with the new dentist.

For her the path was a joy; for her children and grandchildren her song is still singing.

(Top) Wedding photo; (Bottom L) George; (Bottom R) Ethel & Lizzie.

Robert and Ethel with surry standing in front of Custer Hotel. (Bottom L) Ann, Robert, and David taken at Omaha, Nebraska shortly after arriving from Scotland. (Bottom R) Ethel's ninetieth birthday.

(Top) Dr. R.W. Philps in Idaho Falls office, sister-in-law, Lizzie Thompson assisting. (Bottom) Golden Wedding Anniversary – seated: Laura, Dr. Robert, Ethel; standing: Roberta, Ethel, Anabel and David

HIS TRADEMARK WAS A DIAMOND HITCH

With his Stetson perched at a rakish angle on his head, leather gloves on his hands and wearing rider-heeled boots, gangly 18 year old Billy McClure grabbed the stirrup, gave it a snap with the air of the old-timers, he swung astride his saddle-mule.

As the pack train moved out and down the trail, Billy's inner excitement was not visible as he took his position directly behind the most important animal in the pack train, the Bell-mare. (She never strayed from camp, and the mules would always follow her.) The rider of this mare was always the cook who was nicknamed, "Belly-boy," regardless of his age.

To be part of the pack train hired by the government to pack supplies for Colonel Barnard's command of soldiers leaving Boise, made him sit tall and proud. The day progressed with the steady rhythmical sway of mules, click of their hooves striking ground and rock. The easy motion of the mules, had a lulling effect on Billy. His thoughts returned to the events that had led up to this glorious day.

From the time he could remember in Eugene, Oregon, he had smelled the scent of barnyards, of mule sweat-soaked saddle blankets, and leather, and had listened to the startling and raucous braying of mules. Many times he had gone to sleep to the rhythm of them chewing hay, and had ridden long days until at times his young weary body lurched in the saddle.

As he rode along, Billy idly wondered how many trips to various mining camps, including Leesburg and the Salmon River Country his dad had made, and how many miles his dad had ridden through the years, as he made a living for his family.

Now it was he, Billy McClure, riding in those footsteps. This was the summer of 1879, and he was on his way to Custer. In the back country the Sheepeater Indians had gone on a marauding party, robbing and killing the handful of Chinese who were working the dumps at old Oro Grande, on Loon Creek. They had advanced to Custer hiding out in the hills, robbing cellars and killing cows.

As camp time approached, Billy accepted the responsibility of helping unpack the mules, first leading the bell-mare with the mules following, into a semi-circle. When the packs were removed, each mule's gear was lined up in order. (Mornings, the mules would be haltered, led into the same formation and repacked, starting at 3:00 a.m.)

After the mules were turned loose to graze, it was also Billy's duty to help the cook. On his first trip he was a glorified chore boy. Billy unpacked the beans (which had been cooked in salt, drained so they could be packed in the grub box without spilling) set them on the ground by the campfire, and busied himself frying the bacon, while the cook was burying the large dutch ovens filled with soda biscuits in a bed of live coals. When the bacon was fried, Billy emptied the cans of beans into the hot sputtering grease, smashing the beans into a thick past.

With gallons of hot black coffee, dried beans and bacon, hot soda biscuits, and handfuls of dried peaches, apples, prunes or apricots, to quiet the "sweet tooth," the crew felt they "ate high on the hog." (This was also the standard breakfast menu).

After the bone-weary campaign for both soldiers and horses, some 50 of the Sheepeaters agreed to move to the reservation. Others eluded the army. Winter brought the long search to a close, and the campaign ended.

Billy made this life his own. He loved the rough spontaneous laughter of the soldiers, and pack crew, the good natured jabbing of the wranglers and the hidden strength of these mountain men when good judgment was needed. Billy enjoyed the freedom from family restraint. (He was never free from the lovely wild rugged mountain country, where he could catch a string of fish in 30 minutes in the creeks where they camped. Deer tracks were mixed with human tracks near the pack saddle and gear).

As the campaign and summer wore on, the knowledge Bill had acquired on trips when he had accompanied his father paid off. His understanding of mules and care of them was invaluable to the pack boss.

Each night as the packs were pulled, if hair had been rubbed from a spot, indicating a sore was in the making, the aparejoes (thick leather bags filled with willow stocks and hay for padding) were repacked. Sometimes they were strapped around a large fallen log to give them the curve of a mule's back while repadding them, (once a mule had a sore it was virtually impossible to heal on a trip, and at times would have to be unpacked and turned loose). With the constant care most packers came through each pack trip with healthy strong mules.

Searching for a livelihood, it was natural for Billy to dream of buying a string of his own, one mule at a time if necessary. He kept this long-range plan in mind, and the next summer was back in the Salmon River country. Jesus (pronounced by the cowboys Ha'sus) Requetes hired him on as a packer.

Bill hoarded his money, learned to converse in rapid Spanish, and became known as a "man to ride the mountains with." He learned to sleep in snow banks and to tighten his belt when the grub supply was low.

He worked several years for Ol' Casus, packing from all the supply towns. He was no longer the skinny "camp boy" but a dependable, hard working, hard riding man. With these accomplishments, he was beginning to think seriously of settling down. As was the case whenever he hit Boise at the end of a trip, Billy sought out the bright lights and pretty girls. The back country was too far away to pursue this course.

On his last trip to Boise from Yellow Jacket, Billy picked up on a rumor of a gold camp east of Boise called Neil, where some hi-grade ore had been shipped to a mill. He found Casus a packer, turned the string over to him and left for Neil.

It was no hardship in the summer to travel to Boise, which he did quite often. He had met Alice Sakkiee, an attractive brunette with blue eyes, a girl whose father and mother had crossed the plains from Kansas with an ox-drawn wagon and had settled on a 640 acre ranch in Boise Valley.

His courtship went so well that on December 23, 1891, thirty year old Bill and eighteen year old Alice were married in Boise. The housing facilities were scarce in Neil; therefore, they rented a house in Boise. Bill commuted home whenever possible. As he had been a careful spender for years, it was no time until the McClures were owners of a home of their own.

In their modest home all four McClure children were born. Harry, the only boy, was born in 1892; in succeeding years Laura, Jesse and Altha made their appearances.

Bill saw a chance for a good investment and bought 50 head of cows which he grazed on the hills around Neil, riding for them after work.

He never became a dedicated miner. While still mining in Neil, he and a partner bought a ranch on the border of Idaho and Nevada, out of Twin Falls, called Three Creeks. (The buildings were primitive, with only a one-room log cabin, so the family could only live there during the summer months).

This was a good financial move; they built up a good head of cattle, including the 50 head from Neil. The family enjoyed the summers there, and it looked permanent enough that the plans had been drawn up to build a suitable house and outbuildings and to move there. Then the Basque sheepers moved in from the southern part of Nevada, grazing the grass into the ground. Each year more and more came with larger herds. Discouraged, Bill and his partner sold the ranch.

The Thunder Mountain excitement struck Boise. With his expertise with mules and packing he was sure he could make money and bought a string of mules. His ideas were not of gold in the ground, but the gold that could be had for packing needed supplies into such remote country. (At one time he owned three strings of mules, one string of 30 he purchased from a man in Silver City. They hauled everything from huge mill wheels to sawmill carriages and goods.)

The grueling trail into Thunder Mountain took its toll. Horses slipped from narrow trials, mules rolled with their packs. One packer who came in from Oregon and was unfamiliar with such rugged country, tailed his mules. While negotiating a sharp turn on the trail where loose rock was overlaying solid rock, a mule lost his footing, taking the entire string 1000 feet to the canyon floor, losing over half of his mules.

The inevitable happened and the gold became less plentiful. People started leaving Thunder Mountain. With his usual good business sense Bill found buyers for his mule and gear and quit the packing business.

A combination of gold dust fever and an urge for adventure caused Bill to make a decision to go to Alaska, even though it was 7 years since the Klondike strike. He was following a hunch there must be lots of gold that had not been discovered.

With light heart he left for the North Country, knowing he had left his family with a comfortable home and plenty of money and provisions.

Bill was there only a year. He found single life was no longer appealing to him, as he missed his family. Prices were high, gold was not "everywhere," so he caught the last ship out in the fall and came home to Boise, discouraged with life there, but jubilant that he had seen the great raw country.

After much discussion, the McClures decided to look for a ranch. They headed for the Salmon River country in a white-topped buggy hitched to two saddle horses. While Bill drove along with Alice at his side, his happiness was apparent as he fondly slipped his arm around her, and laughed out loud at the kid's antics,. It was great to be home.

The family almost decided on the old Nick Johnson Maraffio place, but Alice spied a large rattlesnake in the road just before they drove through the gateway. If the ranch had been paved with gold, it wouldn't have changed her mind. That snake was BIG!

They drove to another place they had heard about on Squaw Creek. In August the cattle were fat on the rich mountain grass, the place was green and secluded (a blessing to Bill, but a disaster to Alice). They paid the old fox, Frenchman Joe Guthrie, for his squatter's rights and made the move to Squaw Creek in the fall of 1906. They stocked the place with 50 head of cattle and fixed up the old cabin to accommodate the family.

Then winter struck. Not a rock or sagebrush was visible on the hillsides, and the cattle had to be trailed out to be fed in the lower valley.

The baby Altha became worse. (Since the winter when Bill had been in Alaska, all the kids had been ill with high fevers and racking coughs, and had been bedfast for weeks. The rosy-cheeked baby had not made the fast recovery of the three older children. Instead, she seemed to grow thinner and paler each day. The doctors had been called time and again, would only shake their heads and tell Alice they could do nothing for her as her heart had been damaged with the scarlet fever. Now the extreme cold weather, and tight, small house seemed to make it harder for Altha to breathe. In the weeks and months ahead six year old Altha would dress for the day, but would often play for a short time and then recline on the bed, trying to keep up with her school work. When the longed-for spring came, she was never again well enough to romp and play.

The combination of the first bitter winter and the nagging fear for their child, left a dislike for the ranch in Alice's heart. She was never able to overcome it.

The McClures stayed with the up-and-down struggle of cow raising and ranching for 22 years. The family grew, attended Clayton School taught by Miss O'Day. They enjoyed friendships with the neighbors, attended school functions, box socials, spelling bees and joined their neighbors in funerals and weddings.

In 1929 they sold the ranch to Jimmy Ennis. At last they had ready cash. Alice had heard of a renowned doctor in Seattle who specialized in the functions of the heart; Alice and Altha went to Seattle and lived there two years.

Their fears were confirmed; Altha's heart was greatly enlarged and was inoperable. Rheumatic fever, followed by scarlet fever had taken its toll. There was no relief for her condition; it was a sad journey home.

During the summer the McClure family moved to Custer where Bill and Harry had a mine on Custer Mountain. During the months they spent there in the summer, they took out enough gold, even in the depression time, to keep the family comfortable. The family had dwindled to Bill, Alice, Harry and Altha. Laura and Jesse were married and in homes of their own.

Altha gradually became weaker and her suffering greater. Her poor weak body had no resistance left; she died when she was 40 years old.

Bill, Alice and Harry continued to go to Custer for many years -- always moving up when the hills were covered with the green velvet of new grass, with lupine and dandelions waving in the breeze. They bade farewell to the friendly squirrels and chipmunks when the creek began to freeze over in the fall.

In 1948 Alice's foot became inflamed and tender. Then the inevitable happened; her diabetic foot became infected. Harry took her to Pocatello where leg amputation above the knee was performed. One month later she again had surgery. This time her body would not withstand the shock. On May 11, 1948, the blue-eyed girl from Boise who had followed her Mountain-Man where he had led, now took the lead.

Alice was buried in the Boise Valley she loved.

Bill lived to be 92 years old. The tough old "boot" had ridden narrow trails to gold towns and was the namesake of a trail into Thunder Mountain. He had thrown a diamond hitch when he was 12 and played "cops and robbers" for real when he was only 18. Bill had also tried ranching, cowboying, and mining. He was a considerate lover, good father, and kind neighbor who could spin yarns with the best of them.

He became a bed-patient several days before he succumbed. Bill lost track of reality and was again riding the trails of his youth, cussing and talking in Spanish with Casus. He even wanted to go "adventuring" again and said, "Harry, I think I'll take a little trip but I'll need some money." Harry asked him, "Well, Dad, how much do you think you're going to need? He replied, "Well, I think I could make it on a hundred dollars." So Harry counted out the money and placed it in his hand. As he lay contemplating his trip, the money slowly fell from his relaxed hand. The "wrangler" was packing on.

McClure family: (front) Laura, Altha, Jessie, Alice, (back) Bill and Harry.

Bill McClure (center figure) on his saddle mule, mounted ready to trail into Thunder Mountain. The man with his back to camera is Ben Caswell. Caswell brothers discovered Thunder Mountain. (Bottom) Packing up to Leave camp.

Throwing the Diamond Hitch. (Bottom) Alice in front of Boise home.

Harry McClure and friend Tom Horton in ghost town Custer. (Bottom nearing trails end, LtoR) Bill McClure, 87, packer; Jess Hailey, 90, cowboy and woodsman, the town of Hailey his namesake; Jim Agnew, 78, ex-sheriff of Ada County; Frank Pinkham, 73, rancher, Boise Co.; Russ Bryn, 71, Secret Service agent.

THE SWEDISH SOJOURNER

Ellen Louise Olsen, child of the seacoast, was born September 27, 1867, at Torekow, Sweden, where the sea regularly swept the shore, and the wind caused the breakers to rip and roar.

From early childhood she had watched the sea for as long as she could see the bobbing of the vessel that was taking her Papa and three brothers away. As the time neared for them to sail home, she joined her mother in the eternal, fearful watch for masts on the horizon. With the first sightings, life became a frenzied mixture of joy and prayer, making ready the welcome home.

As the ship settled into the slow wash of anchor, the families descended to the shore in a jubilant group, shouting and waving, some blowing kisses on the wind, and some standing silently with bowed heads, giving thanks to God for the safe return of their loved ones once more.

As her Papa and older brothers, with duffel bags swinging from their shoulders, strode up the beach, they were surrounded by Ellen, her mother, two younger brothers and a sister all shouting, laughing and crying together with the men petting and hugging their families.

All special dishes of food that had been planned for their return was quickly put to boiling and bubbling. The warm smell of favorite foods and home was a luxury the men looked forward to from voyage to voyage.

After the evening meal, the younger children cleared the dishes while Ellen's mother bustled around putting hassocks under tired feet and clucking happily at her brood.

As bedtime approached for the children, the sharp sound of the door-knocker would resound through the house time and again, announcing the arrivals of sea-going cronies. They had come to visit until the wee hours of the morning, boisterously telling tall tales with the strong pithy language of the sea, frequently raising their glasses.

As the men started to gather it was a signal for the children to be shoo'ed upstairs, supposedly so their tender young ears would not be exposed to the rougher language.

The older brother knew better as they in their time enlarged a peephole near the chimney where eyes could see the scene below and ears could hear the stories of the sea. Occasionally one of the brothers would stare at the ceiling and slyly wink.

This was Ellen's life until she had passed her tenth birthday. Then the sea claimed its own. Her colorful father and happy brothers no longer trooped up the beach. The last long watch was finally given up, and the sorrowful families stoically accepted their defeat by the monster.

Ellen's father had been captain of a rather large merchant ship; so not only the Olsen family was left destitute. Ellen's mother turned their home into a boarding house and was able to eke out a living for her family with the help of her children.

What a change from former days of extravagant gifts of silken shawls and trinkets from France. Still Ellen was a happy girl; popular among her friends. She had a becoming smile that drew people to her, and she could thing of things on the spur of the moment that brought the spark which made a person entertaining. Her clothes were no longer made from the imported woolens and linens from France, but nothing could change her rich personality.

Ellen was 17 when her mother's friend from America came home to visit. She talked of the small town where she lived and of the opportunities for young girls to make a good living as cooks and serving girls at the various boarding houses and hotels. Since money was very scarce at their home, Ellen soon began dreaming of accompanying Christine Calvin back to America. After much discussion it was decided Mrs. Calvin's sister, Elsie Tennel, who was owner of the Challis House could be Ellen's sponsor. Kind relatives gave Ellen enough money to purchase the tickets.

When the day arrived for departure, everything Ellen owned was packed, including one keepsake from her father -- a beautiful silk shawl. Her many friends trooped to the shore, showering her with gifts and flowers.

As Ellen's friends each wished her every happiness and pled with her to write and send pictures, her mother stood quietly to one side with tears silently sliding down her cheeks. She knew she was also giving this child to the sea -- perhaps not to the depths, but to some far horizon. With despair she felt she would never see her again. The sharp blast of the first warning whistle signaled the friends to stand back as Ellen bade her family farewell. With heavy heart her mother put her arms around this joyous light-of-her-life daughter; then unable to endure more she turned her back on the sea and made her way home.

As the ship nosed into the sea, the figures of her two little brothers plus her friends, was a vision Ellen was never to forget.

When the ship steamed into New York Harbor, the excitement on board ship was a high pitch. Ellen was eager to disembark and start living the life of an American.

She stayed with some Swedish friends who lived in Brooklyn. They visited late into the night. The Brooklyn friends were eager for news of relatives and friends at home.

Ellen and Christine stayed for two days. Ellen was shown as much as could be crowded into such a short time. Then they boarded the train for the West. She found her lack of communication could be made up by her ready smile and happy air.

Finally the last part of her journey began. Ellen left Blackfoot by stagecoach, and Mrs. Mulvaney from Bayhorse was also making the journey. She helped Ellen feel at ease and started showing her objects and telling her the English word for them. Her thirst for knowledge of the English language kept her on this assignment until she had learned to both read and write English with ease.

Mrs. Mulvaney and Mrs. Kate Cameron were friends, and she knew Kate occasionally took in people who needed a home. She suggested Ellen go with her to see what could be found. It was soon arranged for her to stay there until she could establish a place for herself.

Ten days short of her 18th birthday, this Swedish girl had made the transfer from life governed by the happenings at sea, to inland where the ocean was a far-off memory.

After settling in at Mrs. Cameron's, Ellen went to work for Mrs. Elsie Tennel at the Challis House (this building is still being used, now as "The Hub"). Ellen worked long hours, six days a week and helped some on Sundays. Struggling with the communication barrier, homesickness would occasionally engulf her. As time went on, her happy way of making friends soon helped her with her longing for her mother and family. She had also found a very close friend. Ruth Hosforn, who was also of Swedish descent. They became known as the "Two Little Swedes."

Ellen was unhappy working for Mrs. Tennel. When she heard of better wages and better hours at the boarding house at Bayhorse, she went to work up there.

She had now been making her own way for two years and each payday Ellen carefully tucked away every penny she could spare to send home to her mother. (She not only sent money to her mother, but saved enough to send fare for her brothers to come to America. After she had accomplished this, Ellen and the boys sent money home for the rest of their mother's life.)

A boarding house was a good place to meet the young men of the country. Ellen's happy disposition and neat appearance were deciding factors in having male companionship whenever she chose.

After she met the young manager of the Pfeiffer store in Custer, Ellen no longer accepted other engagements.

Charles A. Pfeiffer and Ellen were married when she was 24 years old, December 13, 1890, in Challis, Idaho.

Following the ceremony, they left for Custer. There her new life began. Ellen had spent all her teenage years and early twenties working for someone else. Now she blissfully managed her own home and made it a home where her husband was happy to be, and where the neighbors also enjoyed their hospitality

The birth of their Adelida was a happy occasion. In the ensuing years three more children were born to them. Their contentment with their home and surroundings was reflected in the loving pet-names they bestowed on their children. The hum-drum names of Adelida was lovingly changed to "Lida," Frank Malren to "Buzz", Gladys Barbara to "Cookie" and Charles to "Bunny."

The Pfeiffers had at first rented a house in Custer. As the family grew they both wanted to own their own home so they bought a house next door. Many Sundays and evenings Charles worked to repair and enlarge it. He added a kitchen and built a large storage shed out back.

By now the store was not prospering, and Charles had been bitten by the "goldbug." He lent an ear to every down-and-out prospector in the region and grubstaked them by the dozens. Hoping someday to share a half of a rich lode that would surely be found on his "stake." The financial drain and people drifting from Custer caused the untimely closing of the store.

Then Charles went to work at the Custer Mill. When it closed down he found work at the Sunbeam Mine Mill. His job was to scrape the almalgam from the steel plates.

The only lack Ellen had ever felt in her life was that of education. She felt she may have been "looked down on" in a sense because she had had to make he way with menial tasks, and she wanted none of that for her children.

It was a real sacrifice to send both girls through the teachers Norman School at Albion, and Buzz also attended one year there. (Ellen would not allow the girls to help with expenses by waiting on tables or making beds.)

The Pfeiffers family spent 24 years in Custer and Sunbeam area. The snow and cold were were no bother to Ellen since she was raised in similar country. However when the tops of the fence posts began to show, everyone knew the eagerly awaited spring was on it's way.

The Custer years were enjoyable years. Friends were always dropping in for a friendly cup of coffee, but generally stayed to partake of a meal with a rousing game of whist to top off the visit.

While the kids were growing up it seemed there were more like a dozen Pfeiffers instead of four kids, as some of the neighbors were always staying overnight helping to pop corn or make fudge in the kitchen. They came through the door with hats pushed back on their heads, and glowing cheeks from the cold as they skiied down the slopes of Custer.

When the family was grown and gone from home and the clanking of the mill machinery had stilled, the town of Custer joined other silent towns. Then the Pfeiffers moved to Challis where they had purchased the "Shot Tower." Ellen again made it a cheery home with gay curtains at the windows and the warm scent of freshly-baked cakes or breads issued from the house.

After Lida had received her teacher's certificate, she had gone to Minidoka to teach. There she married the druggist and become the mother of a little baby girl. When her little girl, Ellen, was one year old, tragedy struck the family. Lida became very ill. No medicine seemed to make her condition better. She finally passed away after a long illness. (After her death an autopsy was performed. They discovered she had been the victim of a brain tumor.) Little Ellen was raised by an aunt.

The Pfeiffers enjoyed their years in Challis. Their remaining children married, and both boys settled here. Bunny owned and managed a store. Buzz had a good position with the Forest Service. Gladys spent many years as a teacher.

In February 27, 1936, the little Frenchman (Charles Pfeiffer) from Sacramento, California, whose parents had immigrated from Alsansce Loraine, suffered a heart attack and was laid to rest in the Challis Cemetery.

Three years later, November 5, 1939, at the age of 72, the "Pretty Little Swede," finished her mission.

The girl who had shared lonely vigils watching for a father and brothers who never returned; who tearfully bade her family and friends goodbye at the water's edge; who had strongly convinced her children to pursue an education; and had mastered the English language while successfully managing a home and family, was off on another journey.

ELLEN PFEIFFER'S LETTER

"I was born in Torekow, Sweden on September 27, 1867 and left Sweden September, 1884. I traveled by steamer train and stage. Once of the outstanding incidents of the trip took place after we took on the Irish passengers. We never had potatoes served again on the voyage. I left Sweden because it seemed like a good idea to come to America and send money back to my family.

I arrived in Challis September 17, 1884 and made my home with Mrs. Kate Cameron and through her patience and kindness, I learned a lot of useful things, such as cooking, serving and even how to take care of babies.

The next spring I made my home with Mrs. Ida Baxter (now Mrs. Job). We had a lot of fun together, being about the same age. It seemed like we played more than we worked. I got married December 13, 1890, to Charles Pfeiffer, and lived in Custer for twenty years. Then we moved to Challis in 1910 where

I am now living. I have made lots of friends and have many kind neighbors. I hope to live here a long time yet.

In the year 1884 one of my mother's friends made a visit home from America. Through the influence of Mrs. Christine Calvin and my kind relatives and Mrs. Tennel who all helped me financially, I was able to make the journey to the U.S.A.

I left Sweden the first of September, and my girlfriends and boyfriends followed me down to the boat and loaded me down with flowers, more than I could manage to take care of. It was heartbreaking, but I had to go through with it, too late to back out then.

In Gotteborg we got on a steamboat as far as Liverpool, England. There we boarded a large liner to take us across the Atlantic. We were a week coming over. I stayed two days in Brooklyn with my friends; crossed the Brooklyn Bridge twice. Thought it was wonderful.

Next day I got on the train on my way to Idaho.

I don't remember much about the journey. It seems more like a dream.

All I remember is that there was always some kind person that looked after me, until I arrived in Blackfoot. There I met Mrs. Mulvaney from Bayhorse. We traveled together to Challis. I was very glad of her company. It was a long lonesome ride.

        Ellen Olson Pfeiffer"

Charles A. Pfeiffer, manager of the Pfeiffer store in Custer
Ellen Louise Olsen Pfeiffer, Swedish immigrant

Lida Pfeiffer, lost to the family in her early twenties; (Top R) Gladys Barbara "Cookie", teacher for many years; (Bottom L) Frank Malren "Buzz", Forest Service employee; (Bottom R) Charles Michael "Bunny", store owner and manager.

Ellen & Bunny just finished spreading hay on snow for the chickens.

Pfeiffer home in Custer.

(Top) School children on front porch of the Custer school house, including Pfeiffer children.
(Bottom) Young Lida with friend "Tuff" McGown in Custer.

(Top) In Custer - Gladys Smith with pet cat. Notice the snow almost up to the eaves on the cabin.
(Bottom) Ellen Pfeiffer was a fun-loving lady, and when there was a party, she was always invited. She is the 1st lady from the left.

CHILD OF TRAGEDY

With the closing of the cabin door, 12 year old Amanda Johnson had the feeling the life she knew was ending. Slowly stumbling to the wagon piled high with all their worldly goods, she climbed to the high seat and took the reins from her mother. Simultaneously she flicked the reins and spoke to the horses . . . he wheels began to roll. As the grinding noise of the wheels struck the rocks, Amanda's thoughts turned to despair. She kept her face averted, and behind the poke of her bonnet the tears silently fell. The wind seemed to tug and pull at her poor thin mama as the wagon bumped and swayed over the rough road. Amanda tried to think of the future, but her memories kept getting in the way -- playing in the sun with the happy sound of the river in the background . . . the wonderful feeling of happiness when her mother married her new papa, Louis Kester, (her own father had been killed in a saloon brawl when she was a baby). She enjoyed having a papa to love and care for her . . . to pet her when she was sick, to follow wherever he went. She had watched them build a new home with the bedroom snug and warm dug into the hill.

The heavy smothered feeling was again threatening to engulf her as she thought of the time two months ago when the neighbors had stood with hats off, outside their door, and told them her step-papa was dead . . . killed by a friend. Her frail Mama had grasped the door frame for support, and slowly started to fall saying, "Not again. Please God, not again!"

Now they were leaving the only real home Amanda could ever remember. Of course she loved big Grandpa Olsen and her jolly Grandma. It would be nice to be petted and loved by them. Still she longed for the way things had been.

Tragedy was not through with Amanda yet. One month after moving to her grandparents' home, Amanda was awaken by her mother's tubercular cough changing to a gurgling sound. She hastily lit the lamp only to find her young mother's face smeared with frothy blood, and the bed clothes were slowly turning red. Amanda's scream brought the grandparents. They, too, stood helplessly by while the wracked body of their daughter, Anna, released its hold on life and lay still.

Now Amanda was truly an orphan. Her young heart felt heavy as she helped her sorrowing grandmother prepare the 34-year old Anna for her grave. They dressed her thin body in her prettiest Sunday dress, and Amanda curled her hair the way she had loved to see her wear it. As the long line of wagons filed behind the hearse paying homage to this young Swedish immigrant, Amanda remembered the stories her Mama had told her of her home at Goetenburg, Sweden.

The Johnsons and a group of young married people had decided to make their home in a western frontier town in America. Anna had spoken of the terrible ordeal in the hold of the ship on the voyage to America. They were treated little better than animals with the many immigrants crammed body to body in a small airless space. They had not had enough to eat, and no privacy. The people crowded themselves even more to make room for the pregnant women and for Anna who had tiny Amanda. Because of the immigrant's ignorance of the English language, the ship's crew treated them with contempt, thinking of them as "dumb Swedes." It was not difficult for the immigrants to hear the derision in their voices.

The voyage took two agonizing weeks with young children crying, sick and frightened, or some too frightened to cry. Others of the group were sick from the food, lack of sanitation, the ever-present sway of the ship. The prayed-for time arrived: shore was sighted. The weak were helped from the ship.

This group of immigrants were destined for Franklin, Idaho. However, they were dissatisfied with the conditions there and came to Custer County. The Johnsons, together with 2-month old Amanda, settled on a small place along the Salmon River. These were the memories that stalked Amanda. Now only she was left to fulfill her parents' dream.

Amanda lived with her grandparents for a year. when Mrs. Strand (owner of Challis House and a distant relative) offered her a job for her room, board, and clothing, she accepted. There she lived for five years -- milking cows, cleaning house, washing dishes, and waiting on tables. She attended school in the winter time.

September 1896 was a beautiful month, but Amanda saw little of the outdoors; it seemed to her she was always engaged in household chores. As she wearily ascended to her room to freshen up for serving supper, she rebelliously considered packing her mother's old clothes-bag and leaving. Instead, she poured the large wash bowl full of tepid water ... took a hasty bath, and dressed again in a fresh gingham dress with a white ruffled apron. As she leaned toward the mirror to secure a gold pin on the front of her collar, her reflection showed a slender, blue-eyed girl with honey-blonde hair worn in a becoming coiffure, clear complexion and even white teeth.

With a last touch to her hair she left her room and hurriedly went to the dining room. She had no idea what a pretty picture she presented as she circulated among the tables quietly replacing empty bowls and filling cups. As she neared the end table, an extremely handsome man with dark brown hair and eyes and a mustache caught her attention by his winning smile and nice manners as he accepted a refill of coffee. As she was placing dessert on the table, he quietly asked her if she would visit with him when her work was finished. It seemed to her she had spent half of her life refusing such suggestions but something about this man with the tender sensitive mouth caused her to consent.

With the completion of her work, Amanda was in high spirits as she closed the door on the dark rooms and stepped out into a beautiful evening. At the edge of the board walk sat that handsome John Bowman in a new light buggy with a fine looking horse hitched to it. As they slowly drove along the countryside, they became acquainted by telling each other about themselves and their families.

Amanda related the tragedies she had endured. What she wanted from life and her determination never to marry a Swede. He chuckled to himself. He never bothered to tell her his father left Sweden as Peter Neilson and landed in America as Peter Bowman. He did tell her of the struggle the family had when they first arrived. The kids were dispatched to the neighbor's place during butchering time. There they would catch the blood of the animals, taking it home where their mother made blood pudding. He also told of the time his father tramped fifty miles to get some free potatoes. John's mother peeled them with thick skins, cooked the potatoes and planted the peelings. Somehow they survived that first winter. Next year they planted a large garden and from that time had made good.

He told her of his life from the time he attended the country school in Iowa, to leaving home for western adventure at age 20 with his friend, Charley Danielson. He explained their travel from northern California in 1887 to Nevada, then to Pocatello, Idaho. However, John was still interested in the mining industry, so they came on to Challis. Since he had been raised on a farm and was familiar with stock, he had no trouble securing a job with Jesus Urquides, who owned a string of mules, packing machinery and supplies over the trails into the back country. He reminisced about an unbelievably heavy load: a cable one and one-fourth mile long and one and one-half inch in diameter. It was a tramway cable. Going along sharp curves, a mule would occasionally be dangling in the air as the cable would not bend around a curve. They were also the packers who packed in a 14' diameter flywheel in two pieces. This flywheel had a 4' face and was made of cast iron. Another trip contained the 20-stamp mill; each stamp weighed 600 lbs. and each was 10' long. He was in town this season because he had saved money and bought a half interest in the Black saloon.

This buggy ride was one of many, and as their acquaintance grew, their friendship deepened into love. On August 15, 1897, 27 year old John Aaron Bowman and 18 year old Amanda Sengried Johnson were united in marriage by the Congregational minister in Challis.

Tenderhearted John rented a small neat cabin in Challis and

painstakingly filled it with nice furniture. Amanda hung pretty lace curtains at the windows and placed gay, painted cans with geraniums on the windowsills. She daily scrubbed the wide board floors with hot lye water to keep them snow white and scattered bright braided rugs on them.

Here in their honeymoon cabin their two boys were born -- Dewey on July 4, 1898, and Felix on January 15, 1900.

While her house shone with the love of a fine housekeeper, Amanda at first found cookery trying. She had cooked very little for her mother, and after moving to the boarding house, the Chinese cooks had performed these duties. Her first cake that she proudly carried to the table slanted dangerously and was depressed in the center. As John forceably cut a piece of it, he said with a twinkle in his eye, "Amanda, honey, where is the axe?" She gave him one stricken glance and dissolved in a flood of tears. With a contrite husband to console her she was soon her sunny self again.

In the spring of 1901 the Custer Mill stretched from its long sleep, and the shrill whistle and noise of the grinding machinery was heard in the crisp air -- music to the miner's ears. John made a trip to Custer and immediately wanted to move there. Amanda was reluctant to leave their cozy home but glady joined John in his search for adventure.

John went to work as a mule skinner, hauling cord wood for the hungry boiler at the mill. When fall came, the happy family moved up on Luck Boy hill into another two room cabin with a woodshed lean-to. Here Amanda happily cared for her handsome husband and babies. They melted snow for their water supply and washed clothes under trying conditions. Amanda gave the food she prepared what zest she could from the limited variety of spices available. John left early each morning, and returned 12 hours later at night.

At the end of the winter Amanda was ready for a change of scene and some type of entertainment. One day she suggested to John that they leave the babies with friends and walk the one and one half miles down to Custer. John, who realized the loneliness Amanda had endured, was ready to join her in this quest.

When John finished his shift, Amanda had his bath ready and clothes laid out for him. With haste he prepared for the evening on the town. As they closed the door behind them, John grabbed her hand and together they half ran, half walked the distance down the hill laughing and singing as they went.

Time seemed to have wings as they joined in the good visit with friends. At 11 o'clock they reluctantly gave their farewells and started back up the moonlit trail, only to find the crust on the snow had softened, causing them to sink to their knees with each step. After a tremendous struggle, they exhaustedly opened the door of their home and fell on the bed.

That fall they moved down to Custer. What heaven it was to be able to walk on even ground and have their own home again! This time John went to work as the boiler tender at the mill. Since they lived a short distance from the mill, on many occasions the family had great fun taking their lunch to the mill and eating with John. Amanda would bring big juicy steaks (if they happened to have them), potatoes and bread. They broiled them on a long handled grill over the coals of the broiler. What a great way to have a picnic.

In the summer of 1904 the ore in the Lucky Boy was becoming low grade. The roar and clamor of the 25-stamp mill ceased, and an uneasy eerie silence settled over Custer. As the company intended to rework the old tailing dump, John was employed in the cyanide plant. Even this came to an end.

The Bowmans left Custer on a cold October day. Their destination was Pearl, Idaho. Already the snow was piled high. The runners on the sled squeaked as they slid along toward Clayton, 30 miles away. It was to be the first stop. Even the buttoned-down curtains and heated rocks at their feet were unable to stop the penetrating cold. After several hours they reached Clayton -- a warm station with delicious food.

On the second day the trip was made to Challis. There they stayed several days visiting with friends and relatives. From Challis they traveled by stage to Blackfoot where they boarded a train to Pocatello, then on to Boise. There they stayed overnight with Mrs. Strand's daughter, Mrs. Fennel.

The town of Pearl was 25 miles from Boise on roads similar to the mountain ones from Custer to Challis. The Bowmans rode there in a high wheeled coach with leather springs pulled by four horses. The arrival of the mail stage was an exciting event for the news-starved mining people. The Bowmans were also warmly welcomed.

John found a small abandoned cabin to move into. Having no furniture, he made a cupboard by placing two bins (flour and sugar) side by side with doors underneath for pots and pans. The top was a work table. He was able to acquire a table and four chairs. In his spare time he tore down an old boarding house he bought for $25. This he reassembled into two 12x14 rooms, making their home a nice four room house. (This house still stands basking in the sun after 70 years of time.)

At Pearl the boys attended a two-room, two-story school heated by a pot bellied stove on the first floor and by a large drum through the stove pipe on the second floor.

No matter how poor in wealth the Bowmans were, they never lacked for humor. John inveigled his friend Charley Danielson to causally let it be known around town that the new lady Mrs. Bowman was from Sweden and could understand no English. Then he hid behind buildings and peeked around and watched as Amanda went shopping. As she met people on the street, her face would light up with her lovely smile, only to turn to bewilderment, as everyone she met would nod their heads and pass on by.

After two trips to town the joke was wearing thin. The two men were like two naughty little boys each time they happened to glance at each other they would roar with laughter. Amanda suspected she was the root of their mirth and butt of some joke. When they decided to inform her, they tossed a coin to ascertain who was going to confess. When Charley told her the joke, she tried to be angry at them. However, now the hidden look on faces she had met in the last two days had a meaning for her, and she joined the men in this hilarious joke.

It was at Pearl that Amanda started saving money toward a small farm of their own. She bought a milk cow for $50 and started selling milk, allowing the boys to deliver and collect. In a few years she had purchased several cows.

At last Pearl joined all the other abandoned mining towns. From Pearl the family moved to Quartzville. Here one of Amanda's life wishes came true. On December 13, 1917, she gave birth to a beautiful baby girl and christened her Ann Marie.

The family was ready to put down their roots. They withdrew their savings of $6000 and purchased a nice little fruit farm at Emmett, Idaho. The house was in total disrepair. The whole family tackled this project as they had others. The home was soon not only livable, but attractive and homey. They harvested their first crop of peaches that fall -- a full crop of cantaloupes and a crop of green beans. They still felt the need of a pay check, so John continued to work at the mines for a time. Soon after they moved to Emmett both boys married and left home.

Through all their years John and Amanda found delight in the simple pleasures of fishing trips, picnics and visiting with friends. They saved money so the kids could see some of the wonders of childhood such as a Barnham and Baily circus when it came to Boise, and they enjoyed the new world of radio.

The great depression failed to disturb the Bowmans. They were used to the lack of money, so they tightened their belts and ate a little more fruit and a little less meat. They had the discouragement of losing their cherry crop one year, and the peaches froze on the trees another. These material things never daunted them. When the call came in May 1932 that 32 year old Felix was in critical condition from a ruptured appendix, it was with despair that they watched his life drain away.

After John's death, the place lost its value to Amanda. She sold it and moved to Boise. There she kept her independence as long as she was able, then quietly accepted a home with her children. In August 1970 at the age of 91, Amanda joined Felix and John in that last mining town where the mill never shuts down and the vein never pinches out.

NOTE: During the years that John worked at Custer, he worked 12 hour days for $3 per day, every day of the year. His checks would be $90 for 30 day months and $93 for 31 day months.

(Top) Amanda Johnson, age 17 years; (Bottom) Cabin with dugout bedroom, still standing by the side of highway 93 on the old Floyd Black ranch.

John, Amanda, Dewy and Felix Bowman.

Honeymoon cabin of John and Amanda, located in Challis. (Bottom) John Bowman in his later years. Age rested lightly on his shoulders.

MARY, QUEEN OF COURAGE

Mary Larson was born in the land of the Vikings at Helsingborg, Sweden on March 4, 1854.

She -- together with Lars, Sam, Pete and Anna, grew up in a typical Swedish family. When Nels Johnson started calling at their home, singling out Mary and taking her to parties and socials, she ignored the teasing of her brothers (about robbing the cradle because Nels was a year younger) and happily accompanied him.

After a year of "keeping company," they were married at her home. The party, following the wedding, was filled with sounds of the music from accordians, mouth harps, clinking glasses and the stamping of feet kept the rhythm to polkas. The vision of the milling and jostling tall blonde men, and red and blonde-headed girls with bright dresses, was a party only the Swedish people could give. It was a cherished memory for both Nels and Mary.

After the ceremony Mary and Nels drove to their new little home. It had been cleaned and polished by Mary, her relatives and friends. The flames glowed in the fireplace, and the embroidered pillows and knick-knacks that were part of Mary's trousseau, gave a homey touch to the house.

The following year, their home was filled with more delight when their first baby, Andrew, was born. In the next few years they welcomed to their growing family Josephine, Ulga and baby Annie.

In the 1880's the income of Swedish folk who plowed the fields and threshed the grain was not great. The letters sent from America, by the people who had migrated there, were glowing with reports of good wages and splendid opportunities. These letters must have caused Nel's dormant Viking blood to become restless. He was no longer contented with his life as a farmer and felt his age of thirty-three was no handicap to starting a new adventure.

He and Mary endlessly discussed moving. After many sleepless nights, they decided in favor of moving to America. They sold their farm, animals and house and made the necessary arrangements to live at this former home until their departure.

At the time of departure Andrew was a half-grown boy. He had followed in his father's footsteps day after day and had become good help in any task.

That fall his grandfather needed a "hand" with threshing, so Andrew was sent to help. After a hearty breakfast he and his Grandfather Larson hitched the horse to the pole in the treadmill. Andrew took up his position of driving the horse in the circle, keeping him at a steady pace. As the day wore on the horse became slower. Thinking to speed him up a little, Andrew flicked him with a buggy whip. After the end of the whip hit the horse, the tip fell to the side and caught in the tumbling rod. The handle part was sharply flipped upwards and settled in a noose around Andrew's wrist. His fearful scream, as the whip tightened caused his Grandfather to jump from his stand and grab the horse. Nevertheless, a terrible tragedy had happened -- for his arm had been whipped around, tearing the ligaments and muscles, and splintering the bones in his arm.

The ensuing days and nights were nightmares for Andrew and both families. At first his life was in grave danger; but as the days wore on, the dreaded infection did not appear. Andrew's arm started to heal.

As the fear of death receded, the deadline for the passage on the boat that was to take Nels to America was approaching.

It was a sad and silent group that bade Nels "God's speed."

Nels made his way to Custer, Idaho, where friends had gone the previous year. There he procured a job in the Custer quartz mill, and found a little home to rent on the same side of the street as the mill with a nice spring close by.

Meanwhile, Andrew's arm was not completely healed and was causing him a great deal of pain. Whenever he tried to use it, or whenever he lifted anything with it, the arm would become red and swollen and fragments of bone would erupt through inflamed sores.

Because his grandparents felt such remorse, they begged Mary to leave Andrew with them. She knew nothing about doctors in America or how she could care for his arm on the trip over, so Mary gave her consent. (Andrew never quite forgave his parents for leaving him behind. Although he knew it had been for his welfare, he still felt lonesome and forsaken.

The grandparents took wonderful care of him. When he was strong enough, they helped him secure an apprenticeship with a tailor so he might be able to have a profession to support himself. He later came to America to visit his mother, a brother, and a sister which he had never seen. He then settled in Springfield, Ill., where Mary's three brothers had located.

The great day arrived when Nels finally helped Mary, Josephine, Ulga and Annie from the stage in Idaho. That day was the highlight of his life. He had found pleasure in his new work and friends, but now with his family, Nels was complete.

Their Custer home was a happy one. The favorable reports of Andrew's apprenticeship, and healing of his arm gave them great happiness. Also, Custer had its share of Swedish people who helped the Johnson family to make adjustments to the new country and language. The three little girls joined the children in school and play and were soon conversing in English with ease.

One morning when Mary was preparing breakfast, she noticed an unusual blemish on her chin and across a part of her cheek. She also was becoming nauseous, and was forced to lie down. In the following days, her fever rose. She was only partially conscious at times. When a doctor arrived he diagnosed her illness as Erysipelas.

During the first week of her illness, the weather had warmed -- causing the steep, snowcovered mountainside to become unsettled and shifting. Because of his steady concern over Mary, Nels had failed to notice the danger signs. As his family lay sleeping one night, a snowslide broke loose, gained momentum as it roared down the steep mountainside, and brought with it a burden of trees and debris.

Nels was awakened by the roar and vibrations in the cabin. Sensing the great danger, he jumped from the bed and gathered his stricken Mary in his arms. As he straightened up with her, the avalanche struck their cabin, bringing the door before it and forcing a board between them.

Nels and Mary were standing buried alive. The board that had been forced between them gave each enough air to breathe, and the mishap door frame kept some of the weight of the snow mass above from crushing them.

The three little girls in the back bedroom were crushed in their beds. A huge stump had plunged through the roof and completely covered them. (Until a few years ago this stump could be seen at Custer in the spot where it had rolled.)

Mary was partially conscious. She could only think of work when she heard the mill whistle screaming above them. It was the call to alarm, but she kept repeating over and over to Nels: "You will be late to work!"

Frantically, the neighbors dug and shouted. At long last the searchers could hear a faint, hollow sound that guided their shovels as they dug.

Neither Nels nor Mary were hurt. Mary recovered from the Erysipelas, and her heartache was eased somewhat when she gave birth three months later to a fine, healthy son. They christened him George.

Nels had now been working in the "dry crush" mill for seven years. During this time Mary had noticed that many of the men who worked in the mill had coughing fits that were progressively getting worse. When Nels started the "jackhammer laugh," she became frightened and begged him to quit the mill. Feeling his strong, vital body weakening with the ever-present coughing, he finally consented in 1894. The Johnson family moved to Challis where their last child was born -- Lillian Johnson Millick.

For Mary, it was a difficult sight to witness her once-strong farmer husband wasting away. He could no longer lie in bed. He spent the last few months of his life sitting and sleeping in a chair. It was a burden to him to know that his wife was earning a living for them by washing and ironing, and occasionally helping neighbors as a midwife.

Nels continued to weaken and just after his 42nd birthday his respiratory system failed. He was laid to rest on April 5, 1897.

(The following is the account taken from the Silver Messenger of April 13, 1897):

> "Dr. Jacobsen, in the presence of a few witnesses held an autopsy in Challis last week over the remains of Nels Johnson, whose death was supposed to have been caused from working in the Custer Mill. Many who have worked in this mill have died young, and it has always been a question of vast interest to the public to know what was the direct cause of their death.
>
> This mill in question is what is termed a 'dry crush' mill from the ore which is inhaled quite freely into the lungs and the conclusion was the cause of death. The post mortem examination held today proves this theory to be false. The examination showed no dust whatever upon the lungs, but the lungs were in a terrible condition: both were entirely dead. One had grown to the back and both were encased with a hard, green substance which we are told is caused from inhaling chlorine gas. The heart was in good condition."

Now Mary turned her full time to working for her family's support. She knew there was more washing and ironing to be done in Custer; so she moved her family back there. The Johnson kids once more roamed the hills which they loved, searching for wild flowers and "pretty rocks."

After Mary had completed a washing she would carefully line George's little wagon with an old clean sheet, deposit the washing in it and wrap the load tightly so dust would not seep into it. George would pull the wagon while Lillie would push. They delivered washing all over town in this manner, even to Senator McBeth's residence, and to the red-light ladies abode (discreetly after dark). The ladies tipped the children very generously.

After Mary had been a widow for four and one-half years and was 47 years old, she met and married a much older man -- Alexander Kluepfer. He was the mechanic and foreman at the Custer Mill for many years. Alexander migrated from Switzerland during the gold rush of 1849 and had come to Custer in 1879, thus making him one of the early pioneers there. They made a comfortable home for each other, and he was a kind stepfather to George and Lillie.

When the mill closed in 1904, Alex left for a gold strike in Nevada. Then Mary and the rest of the family moved to Challis. Alex wrote fairly often and sent what money he could spare.

However, he was getting old and ill health was adding to his worries. Too ill to work, Alex came back to Challis, a old and broken man. He died October 13, 1912, and was buried in the Challis Cemetery.

From this time on Mary worked wherever she could obtain a job. She became a familiar figure at most of the bedsides where a midwife was needed. Between these engagements she could count on steady work at the Drake household, where she helped with all household duties, and even went to their sheep-shearing camp in the spring where she cooked for the shearers.

Through the years she scarcely realized her family was gown until the day her tall son, George, kissed his mother goodbye and headed for the Sunbeam mine where he had been offered a job. (There he met Eva Ellis, who was cooking at the Sunbeam boarding house and married her. When the mine shut down, they moved to Klamath Falls, and both resided there until recently when George went out to feed the Holstein bull at the dairy where he worked. In a fit of rage the bull charged George and fatally gored him. Eva tried to rescue him, but the bull only turned on her and rendered her unconscious. Eva recovered and still lives there, caring for her son who was totally paralyzed from an automobile wreck.).

When Mary rented a log cabin from the Millick family the dirt roof leaked when it rained or snowed; so Earl Millick came to repair the roof. He became attracted to redheaded Miss Lillie and escorted her around to the social functions. In 1913 they were married.

Now Mary was responsible for only herself. She moved into a snug little cabin (directly across from the Community Church) known as the Mandy Beck cabin, and lived there for the rest of her life.

Her profession was almost entirely midwifery. She would have her board and room furnished for ten days, plus $2 a day. She became known to the community as "Ma" Kleupfer.

Her last case was December 9, 1919, when she helped Dr. Kirtley bring Gridley Rowles into the world. On the last morning of her stay Don Rowles asked her, "Ma, how are you this morning?" Mary sadly shook her head and replied, "Donnie, I think you'll have to take me home. I feel poorly."

The neighbors took turns looking in on "Ma." They were worried she would have a miserable Christmas, because of her illness. Lillie and Earl offered her a home with them; but to the last day Mary kept her independence. Friends came by often and brought chicken broth and hot bread and stoked up the stove.

Gradually Mary became weaker, and on March 10, 1920, she joined Nels and her girls.

Her stalwart courage was an example to all who knew her. She "made do" with what she had, and turned any cabin she occupied into a cozy, comfortable home.

Hers was a "peace that passeth all understanding."

(Top) Josephine (left), Ulga Johnson (middle) and Anne (right): The Johnsons whose young lives were snuffed out long ago on a February night by an avalanche, which struck the Johnson cabin. (Bottom) Lillie Johnson Millick.

(Top) George and friend, Ruth Dorgan. (Bottom L) Mary Johnson Kleupter, (2nd from L) Anna Larson Williams, (3rd from L) K.D. Williams - taken in front of the Robinson Bar Hotel when Williams owned the property.

Lillie (as a young married woman) with a group of friends.

JOSIE -- THE GIRL WHOSE FEET
TROD THE PATHS TO GOLD AND SILVER MINES

Josie Mavity Ebberts, who was born January 16, 1896 says,
   "I guess you could have called me a golddust kid, for I was born in Bayhorse and raised in Custer, Idaho; both places are now ghost towns.
   Bayhorse was a roaring mining town with houses and tents, built beam to beam, one grocery store, a post office, a mill, and nine saloons. We lived in two one-room cabins with a dog-trot connecting them.
   My dad, James Thomas Mavity, worked in the Ramshorn mine, way up on the mountain, and only came home once or twice a month. When I was four years old, I rode up that narrow, steep, winding road in a grocery wagon, pulled by two horses and driven by George Hosford. He delivered meat and groceries to the boarding house. My dad was so tickled to see me, he took me down into the mine so I could see where he was working. Then we ate dinner at the boarding house. I remember so well the Chinese cook there, who was called Lee Kong. He said to me, 'Leetle girl, you can't sit on one box, you leetle kid, I put two boxes up for you.' I could hardly wait to get home, I was so full of my own importance of where I'd been and what I'd seen."
Josie continues,
   "My dad's mother died when he was only nine years old. When he was presented with a stepmother, he ran away from home, never went back. In 1862, when he was 18 years old, he enlisted in the Union army and was mustered out at Goldsburg, North Carolina, in 1865. He had received a wound in his shoulder and upper arm that was to give him many painful times. It also left him with the disability of only being able to raise his arm shoulder high. Many times a year this wounded area would become swollen and inflamed, and he would be unable to work until the heated compresses and medication reduced the inflamation."
   From 1865 to 1882 little is known of his life. After 1882, when thirty eight year old James was married at American Falls to fifteen year old Louisa Dee Workman, his life was no longer a mystery. The new couple moved to Bayhorse, Idaho, and through the years they became the parents of eleven children.
Josie says,

"Mama's first two little boys died, then Fred, Mattie, Stella, Happy, Josie, Lucy, Ruth, Arnold and Kate were born. Lucy died when she was two years old and Arnold when he was four months. My mother led a hard life, but a happy one. She took in washing and ironing. She sometimes sat up until three o'clock in the morning, and by an old kerosine light, she would make over clothes for us kids. The clothes had been given to her by Mrs. McBeth or some of the well-to-do people in town."

Money was never plentiful in Josie Mavity Ebberts' early life. Her father followed the mining trade. Once he had tried farming, but was unsuccessful and returned to mining.

About the time Josie was five years old the Ramshorn mine was hitting low-grade ore and was in the process of shutting down. The Mavitys packed up and moved to another mining town, Custer, Idaho. There they lived, by the mill, in a three-room cabin. It was here that the last baby sister, Kate, joined the family.

Speaking of her early life Josie says,

"Both Bayhorse and Custer people were all like one big family. If someone was sick or needed help everybody pitched in. If there was a party everybody was there with family and food. When there was dancing, we little kids would dance until we were all tired out, then we bedded down in a corner on some coats. Mavitys learned to work early. My brother Happy and I took on the janitor job at the Custer school. We got out our own wood, using an old horse to snake the logs down the mountain. Then we cut it up with a cross-cut saw, split and piled it. We built the fire in the stove, cleaned the desks, wiped up the floors each day. We took care of what books the school had and each morning my brother brought in a bucket full of water. (We all drank from a common dipper.) We did all of this for $3.00 a month for each of us.

I also worked for anyone who needed a girl. We kids would go around town and collect all the whiskey flasks we could find and turn them into the store. That was good for a little spending money. I also worked for the Postmistress, Mrs. Morrison. She saved her dishes up all week and Friday after school I would wash, dry and put them away, and clean her house. She paid me fifty cents and my meal.

To help out on expenses, my mother was again taking in washing. She had some colorful characters to wash for. Red McGee was a famous gambler in Custer; she had Mrs. McBeth, who was the superintendent's wife; and she washed for anyone who cold afford to have washing done."

Josie continues,

"It wouldn't be a complete picture of the early days in Custer if I didn't include the redlight ladies. Whenever these ladies were out in public they sort of kept to themselves. We kids knew those ladies were different, but we were too young to know why. We just knew they were good to us, and to anybody who needed help. My folks never forbade us to visit the little houses with the red curtains, and pretty red blinds, but we never did."

It wasn't all work and no play for the kids. When Happy would have a little time between jobs, he'd tell Josie to get the bait and they'd go fishing. She recalls,

"Id catch the perrywinkles off the rocks and in a couple of hours time we'd have all the fish we could string on two willows. Then being a big brother, he'd say, 'I don't have time to clean them.' Cleaning that many fish, I soon lost interest in eating them."

The kids saw tragedy in the raw. They silently watched the slow progress of some miners pulling sleighs; strapped on the sleighs were three Austrian miners who had been caught in a snowslide while coming down from the Charles Dickens mine. The fact that these men had been repeatedly warned not to travel that trail during snow-slide weather made the occasion no less of a disaster. As the victims were being slowly taken toward town, the kids saw a slight movement of one of the men on the sleigh and he tried to lift his arm. However, within minutes he, too, died.

When the low grade ore was beginning to be tapped at the Lucky Boy mine and James Mavity's bad shoulder was taking a toll on his health, he left the mine and hired out for the mail stage driver job. He drove between Robinson Bar and Custer. At the same time, Louisa took the two youngest girls, Ruth and Kate, with her and hired out that summer as the cook at Robinson Bar, a stage stop and guest ranch. This left fourteen-year-old Josie to prepare the meals for her brothers and to take care of the home.

In 1911 in a covered wagon drawn by two horses, Mr. and Mrs. Mavity and a tearful bunch of Mavity kids took to the road again, leaving behind many of their friends.

Josie says,

"Everything we owned was piled on that wagon, leaving very little room for my folks, Mattie, Ruth, Kate, Happy, Fred and me. We slept on the ground, whether it rained or not, and it rained most of that trip to Gilmore, Idaho, another mining town that was to be our home. We girls helped with the meals. We cooked bacon, eggs, potatoes and canned corn. At every meal we made campfire bread by mixing up biscuit dough and putting it in a cast-iron frying pan, held up by crossed sticks next to the campfire. Boy! We kids just loved that bread. Sometimes on that trip, the boys would kill a wild chicken, but mostly we lived on provisions that could be hauled without spoiling. It took us four days to travel that 200 miles."

The barren hillside town of Gilmore was a typical thrown-together mining town of 3000 people . The large amounts of ore produced there warranted the coming of the railroad everyday. Josie recalls,

"There was the part of town called tent-town, a full part of the city made up of tents that had been pitched over board floors. Then there was Ragtown, built in a gulley, so called because it was filthy, with rags, paper and trash everywhere. It was here they made and sold rot-gut whiskey. This was during prohibition days, but they ran full time, twenty-four hours a day, gambling and selling whiskey.

Then there was a row of houses built by the company in the regular town. We lived in one of those two-room houses, all seven of us. It helped that the beds were built against the walls, but the houses were small and the everpresent wind and and cold forced its way into every crack and cranny of the house. Our whole family was sick that winter. If we hung our clothes out to dry on the clothes lines, someone had to continually watch or our clothes would be down the mountain carried away by gusts of wind.

The water was piped to the houses. It froze in November. Then they brought us one barrel of water per week. We melted snow to wash our clothes and clean our house.

Part of the company policy was the use of the company doctor. He visited all of the miners and their families when needed. When James Mavity was laid up with the recurring shoulder infection, Dr. Paul came to see him. After attending to him he looked around and noticed how pale Josie was and said to Mr. Mavity,

"What's the matter with your daughter? She looks ill to me."

Josie remembers,

"I'd been ill most of my life, but down there I

> couldn't seem to get my usual strength back. After a thorough checkup Dr. Paul said, 'No wonder she's sick, I don't know how she's gone on at all. She needs blood.' So he put me on straight iron. It was so strong and would have discolored my teeth by direct contact; so I sucked it through a straw. His diagnosis was correct, for in no time at all I felt like a new person."

As spring broke, James Mavity's health was no better. The boys were tired of fighting the wind, cold, and poor health. A vote was taken and the family decided to move to Challis. This was the last move the family made. They bought a house and James Mavity was hired as deputy sheriff. He was well enough to take the prisoners their meals, clean the jail and take his turn staying there. For this service he was paid $75 per month; and along with his war pension of $75, the family made do.

While Jim was working as deputy sheriff, he was again having trouble with his arm. Dr. Kirtley came to see him, and told him,

> "Jim, I realize you are well up in your seventies, but I think Dr. Hartman and I can relieve some of that pain."

They operated on him on the kitchen table with the rest of the family in the next room. They found the ball had shattered the bone and the fragmented pieces of bone were still grinding against tissue. They removed all of the loose fragments, and Jim lived until December 16, 1924, relatively free from what had seemed a lifetime of pain.

Because of her many illnesses, Josie had missed out on two years of school. However, she went back to school in Challis and finished the eighth grade with several of her old Custer friends who had also moved. While she was attending school she was also working after hours, in the cafes, boarding houses, or anywhere she could earn a few dollars.

While socializing with the young people of Challis, Josie was introduced to Bill Ebberts. He was just home from college where he had won medals for his athletic abilities. He seemed to be able to play any musical instrument, was fun to be around and joined in with all of her friends. Before long they were a twosome, and on November 10, 1914, they were married. Their first home was on Main street -- a log cabin with a dirt roof. It was there that all four of their children were born and also where the four Bradley children joined the family. They were Bill's sister's children. The Ebberts finished raising them.

Both Bill and Josie worked. Josie said of those times,

> "I'd made up my mind that my kids were going to get a high school education. With that in mind I'd get up at 6:00 a.m. and go to the Hazel B. cafe. I'd build the fires, get breakfast, and finish my shift around

2:00 p.m. Then I'd go home, beginning my second job which was washing and ironing for people. Some days I'd iron as many as thirty of those white shirts.

Then the war came along and all three Ebberts boys enlisted. Jack and Bill in the infantry and Joe in the Navy. In a low, sad voice Josie said,

"Jack was killed October 3, 1944, in Germany; Bill was wounded in Casablanca; and Joe was injured in the Pacific.

On Josie's 18th wedding anniversary, November 19, 1932, the Mavity family lost their valiant mother; and in 1952 Josie lost her Bill. He died in a car injury.

Josie summed up her life:

"We Mavitys learned to work. There was no lazy way out. We made do with what we had; we raised good families; and I'd say, when it comes to pioneering, I've done it all."

Four of the Mavity girls: (seated) Mattie, Stella, (standing LtoR) Josie and Kate.

(Top L) James Thomas Mavity; (R) Louisa Workman Mavity; (Center) gave birth to 11 children and raised seven of them. (Bottom L) three young men of Challis (LtoR) Bill Ebberts, Buzz Pfeiffer & Tuff McGown. (Bottom R) Josie.

(Left on snowshoes) James Mavity, friend, and son, Fred.

THE BADGE OF COURAGE

Brownhaired, blue-eyed Mary Price was born on a warm balmy day -- October 2, 1843, at Fillmore, Missouri. It was a time when grievous conflict was prevalent among neighbors; a beginning of a way of life.

Fillmore was on a borderline of the Confederacy and as Mary grew up, she watched and endured the terrors of guerrilla warfare. In 1861 all the bitter strife was forced to a head when war was declared between the states. Men and boys able to walk and pack a gun were gone overnight.

Mary's family had already endured economic reversals and early hardships; but now they were forced to witness bloodshed, vast destruction, and finally confiscation of their property.

During this upheaval in the early part of 1862 some of the men were being mustered out who had become ill or had been seriously wounded. Among this group of men was dark-haired slender-build James L. Kirtley, a young man who had not only suffered loss of health from the war, but had also lost his young wife, while he was gone to war.

The people still at home tried to carry on, and those able to attend faithfully joined their neighbors each Sunday at their places of worship. It was at church that James again renewed his acquaintance with pretty Mary Price whose beautiful smile he found enchanting and whose eyes had a mischievous twinkle.

From the time James asked permission to "keep company" with Mary until the time she became Mary Price Kirtley, April 24, 1862 was a matter of months.

The war was still making heavy demands on the people and country. Now recovered from his war experience, James had no difficulty in procuring a job, but the wages at the hardware store where he worked were barely enough to buy their food. Mary patched their clothes and then put patches on patches.

The only available house the Kirtleys could find to lease was an old drafty one, where the wind easily whistled through. It was here that Mary gave birth to their first little girl in January of 1863. Whether from Mary's improper diet, living conditions, or her worry and strife, this little girl never seemed to thrive. When a contagious flu prevailed in their county, the baby became ill and died. The struggling young couple accepted the tragedy with the stoic calm with which they had endured their previous hardships.

To get away they decided to join a wagon train assembling and leave their strife-torn homeland. They struck out for the gold country. The Kirtleys bought a wagon and team of horses from one of their friends who was leaving for the East because she had lost both her husband and boys in the war. They slowly accumulated the necessities and tools they would need on the trip.

In 1864 while they were making these plans, Mary again gave birth to a vigorously healthy baby girl. With the birth of this baby and the train assembly going forward in good time, the Kirtleys youthful expectations began to take on meaning again.

The war dragged to a close on April 9, 1865 Two weeks later at the crack of dawn the exciting anticipated moment of leaving filled the air. At the crack of his whip the flamboyant leader's command of, "Wagons Ho" rang out. He waved his arm forward; the wheels began to roll.

Mary was not torn between excitement of adventure and leaving loved ones, as some of the young people were, her family was part of the train. Some days of travel were warm and balmy, and the surrounding country green and beautiful. Other days the dust boiled up around the wagon wheels as they crossed drought-stricken country.

The hazards of wagon travel included lack of food at times, sickness and Indian raids. After 93 days on the train, it pulled into Virginia City, Montana. Again the Kirtleys had suffered personal loss. They had left their baby girl buried beside the trail on the prairie -- lost to a disease called camp sickness (a form of dysentery).

Even though their grief seemed overwhelming, the atmosphere at Virginia City was like coming into sunshine. Everyone was wearing reasonably new clothing; seemed to have ready money to spend; and the horses and mules had the slick glossy coats of well-fed animals. Also, the whole camp seemed alive. Glamourous noises and music ricocheted from the hills day and night. Even the crowded condition of people arriving could not take away the exhilarating new world for the Kirtleys.

They bought a claim from a prospector who wanted to follow the glory trail, and pulled their wagon to the makeshift cabin, using the wagon for sleeping quarters and the cabin for cooking.

These were the kind of days that these young people needed -- optimistic talk of strikes to be found tomorrow differed from the Kirtleys yesterdays. Here on their claim at Blacktailed Deer Creek, September 29, 1866, Mary gave birth to their first son -- christened Frank Price Kirtley; named after his father's brother. He was the first white child born in Montana. Although their claim was a poor one, and demanded many hours of back-breaking shoveling, it produced a steady income for Mary and James while baby Frank crowed and babbled from his nearby wooden packing box.

As the news of the Leesburg strike reached Virginia City, people left by the dozens. The man on the claim next to Kirtley's threw his shovel on a pile of dirt, rushed into his cabin, grabbed a flour sack and hastily stuffed it with some grub. He tied his bedroll on the back of his saddle and kicked his horse into a lope. In less than twenty minutes he was gone, leaving only a trail of dust.

The whole town was in an uproar. People were leaving all hours of day and night. The frenzy finally caught up with Mary and James. However, they again carefully stocked the covered wagon with plenty of provisions and tools. They also packed all their clothes, bedding and what few items of furniture they could squeeze into the wagon.

On a bright spring morning in 1868 they followed the stampede. As the Kirtley's team started down the long grade from the divide, the Lemhi valley stretched out before them. The rush of the river and the green patches of grass along the rough road gave them a feeling of coming home. As they drove up to the trading post, James handed the reins to Mary and jumped to the ground. He had the urge to inquire if any placer mining was being done in this valley. As he introduced himself to the storekeeper, he told him of the interest he and his wife felt for the country. As the storekeeper had heard nothing but, "How far is it Leesburg?" for many days he was favorably impressed with this young family and divulged some mining secrets. He told James where he had found some "color" in a creek just below a tall mountain peak he called Fremont Peak.

As James related this information to Mary, she brought her spellbound gaze from this beautiful spot to his face, then eagerly nodded her head in agreement when he suggested they travel to this creek overshadowed by the tall rugged peak.

The Kirtleys homesteaded 80 acres under Fremont Peak and called the creek which fed their placer Kirtley Creek. James built a log cabin, and they began their ranching life. They also built barns and fences and planted their crops and a large garden with the questionable help of baby Frank.

As September approached, Mary again gave birth to another boy who was named Lawerence. Now she had the settled awareness of putting down roots.

James scouted the area several miles above the ranch. He carefully panned the stream and had found good color. He was impatient to be starting his placer.

As fall changed to winter, little Lawerence became feverish and ill. Mary tried all the home remedies she had learned and also sponged the hot little body with cool water -- to no avail. The parents took turns walking the floor with him, back and forth, back and forth, patting his little back. They fought the mounting terror as he slowly weakened and went into a heavy sleep from which he never awakened. After each of these bitter misfortunes, there were times when 24 year old Mary seemed to bog down with grief. She felt she had lived a hundred years.

As the next spring approached, again the Kirtleys had a new baby. This one was christened James. Until Mary was forty years old she gave birth to a new baby every two years (besides Frank and James the children were Kathreine (Kitty), born 1871; Charles Luther, 1872; and Nell, 1875. They again lost a baby in 1877, then Wade Hampton was born in 1879; Isabel Virginia (Belle), 1881; and Francis, 1883.

Instead of despairing at all the expenses as each new baby came to the family, the added babies seemed to enhance Mary, further nurturing her youthful appearance. She had the incentive to build and expand.

After James planted the large garden each spring, he spent more and more time at the place on the mountain. Mary was developing the ranch. She had discovered that any produce she could make or raise could sold at Leesburg.

Mary also had a dream of sending all of her boys to college. She developed a large herd of milk-cows, and churned butter, made cheese, picked loads of green vegetables and packed them into wagons. Then James and one of the lucky boys drove the produce wagons over the hill to Leesburg. A great share of cash derived from these sales was carefully banked for the boys' education.

While James was spending almost all of his time at the placer, Mary was chafing at the smallness of the ranch, which she felt was curtailing her earning ability. In 1882, she accepted the job as the first postmistress of Salmon, and moved the family into town. While working as postmistress, Mary never lost track of her dream of a large ranch. Two years after moving to Salmon, the Kirtleys bought a 640 acre ranch two and one half miles from Salmon.

Here they had enough land to expand and raise feed for the cattle operation. It had a large old log cabin on it. As time went by, they built a home large enough to accommodate the family. This house has 5 bedrooms, extra-large living and dining rooms, a large kitchen and work porch, and a milk house built over a cool stream situated close to the back door. Mary continued her dairy production. (This ranch house is still standing. The exterior has been changed).

The ranch also had a large apple orchard just under the hill and barns, corrals and outbuildings. This new ranch was only 7 miles from the placer mine by way of a trail through the hills, where the boys slipped away as often as they could elude their mother.

At the time the family settled on this ranch, Frank was 18 years old and had helped earn the family income since he had been able to fork a horse or milk a cow. Many times he had worked for the neighbors and had even carried the mail down the river when he was very young. When all other work slackened, he broke horses and helped at the placer. Mary looked to him to help her guide the younger boys.

James sold his placer to a large Salt Lake City company. They hired him as foreman. The company brought out large crews to work, and built a large flume and work buildings. They also built five large houses at the placer site. The largest one, reserved for the owners, consisted of 11 rooms, each room equipped with a large fireplace. The company also built two offices, one with a big vault. After all the building was completed, they employed another large crew of men to work the mill. (Isabel and Francis Kirtley were the cooks one summer.) A large number of these workmen were Chinese. The company worked the placer for three years. Then they left as abruptly as they had come, leaving James as watchman for the silent valley. He lived in two rooms of the large house for 15 years, content to know he had helped provide Mary and the family with a large ranch. While working as their watchman, the company allowed him to continue to work for gold, which he did with the help of several of the Chinese. (One Chinese couple liked the Kirtleys so well they named themselves Kirtley Sam and Mary Sam).

Vivacious and high-spirited Mary joined the Eastern Star just three years after her last baby was born, and was the first Worthy Matron of this lodge, while James was the first Worshipful Master of Lemhi Lodge.

Through the diligence and hard work of all the family, the ranch prospered, but Mary lost a part of her dream. Frank refused to go to college. He was content with ranch life. Wade had been bitten by his father's love for mining. After he attended college, he followed this course for years. He was also auditor and recorder at Salmon for a long time. Still he liked the ranch, so he and his wife went back to the home place. As an added enjoyment they raised race horses. Charles Luther was their fourth living child. When he left Salmon for his higher education he chose the University of Idaho and was one of the four who comprised the first graduating class. His course was in civil engineering. But while he was completing this course he was influenced by two factors: First, it had always made him feel sad when he heard the stories of how helpless his parents had been when they lost their babies. The second factor was the growth of the population in Idaho with so few doctors to care for them. Charles enrolled in Rush Medical College in Chicago, Illinois. He always gave the credit for his success to his early training and discipline of sharing responsibilities of milking, irrigating, punching cows, and helping his father at the mine. Charles was a great source of pride to his parents.

All the children married with the exception of Isabel. By the time she was 25 years old and was thinking of settling down, her beloved mother became ill. She nursed her faithfully for two years.

Mary's seemingly boundless strength began to fail, then she developed pneumonia. As she steadily grew weaker all the children were summoned. Charles, who lived at Custer, made the trip to Challis on horseback, then from Challis to Salmon in a buggy. The trip was made in less than 18 hours. Jimmy and Francis, who were in Custer's back country, were also summoned and went to their mother. James and all eight children were with her. As the saddened group each quietly took turns sitting by her bedside, Mary still endowed them with the magnetic spark of encouragement and the fierce pride she felt for them.

One day short of her 65th birthday, Mary quietly went to sleep. The respect she had demanded from herself and others was shown by her neighbors and townspeople. The funeral cortege was over one-half mile long, honoring this good woman, kind neighbor, and ideal wife and mother.

After James lost Mary, he continued to spend years at the placer as watchman. When his eyes began to develop cataracts, he went to the ranch to live with Isabel. One fall day, after an excursion in Salmon, one of the family took him back to the ranch. As they started to turn down the lane, he said,

> "You've taken enough time with me. Let me out to walk down the lane. I can see well enough for that, and I want to smell the fields as I go."

Realizing he wanted to walk alone, they bade him goodnight and left for town. As he ambled along the lane, his foot caught the edge of the road, causing him to stumble and fall into the roadside ditch. The fall stunned him, and he drowned.

At age 80 James was laid to rest by his Mary on October 15, 1915. The cemetery overlooks beautiful Lemhi Valley, Fremont Peak, their first homestead, the placer claim and the ranch.

This courageous couple's early struggles with poverty, destruction, and grief had only served to give them the fortitude and determination to do the best by each other and their children and to make the most of each day as it dawned.

(Top) Mary Price Kirtley. (Bottom) Son, Charlie, now a doctor.

The Kirtley sisters with friends at a picnic on the ranch.

HORSEBACK MEDICINE IN EARLY CUSTER COUNTY

Wirery, undersized ten year old Charlie Kirtley set the foam-crested, brimming milk pails down on the path leading to the house. While he idly rubbed his back with one hand, his eyes wandered to the mountains. As his gaze lingered there he allowed his imagination to run -- to the busy activity of the placer -- saw his father's hat pushed far back on his head as he bent over the gravel looking for "color." Charlie imagined the noise and laughter of the whitemen joking and their derisive remarks to the pigtailed Chinese.

With a heavy sigh Charlie again took up his burden. The barn-cats and the dog patiently trailed behind him. It seemed to Charlie he was always milking, feeding, chasing, branding, working with cows, or running errands for the big boys. If his mother noticed he was idle, he was whisked to the garden. The rows seemed endless when the hot sun beat down on his back. All he asked from life was to saddle old Jack, splash through the river at a run and head for the placer.

The only times he went willingly to the garden were when the family filled the wagon with vegetables, rhubarb, and gooseberries, to take over the hill to Leesburg. Charlie eagerly helped to pack produce in wet cool grass in the wagon bed. His reward was realized when his father would casually hand Charlie the reins. With the reins in his hands, it seemed to him his small skinny body was ten feet tall, as the high-stepping nervous team accepted his commands. When the wagon neared the edge of Salmon, Charlie would put his hat straight on his head and sit with his back razor sharp and rigid. He was always careful to flick the back of the horses with the reins and sharply command them when they drove through the busiest section of town--mimicking the grown men as closely as he was able.

When the team and the wagon approached Leesburg, men and ladies alike came to the wagon with pans, buckets, and boxes of all shapes and sizes. They were starved for green produce. Charlie nimbly hopped in the back and handed down the vegetables, fruit, cheese, butter and eggs, while his father supervised and accepted the money. In minutes the wagon was empty. Then Charlie was allowed to explore and to visit with his friends, while his father had a friendly drink or conducted business.

The years rolled by swiftly, and the trips to Leesburg were many. After each trip a great share of the money was carefully banked toward education for the four Kirtley boys. Of the family of eight living children, Charlie's mother hoped to be able to send all the boys to college, planning that the girls would marry and have someone to make their livelihood for them.

All the Kirtley children were eager to earn money and worked for other people when seasonal jobs were available. The boys (although small men) were efficient and capable working men, and earned their day's pay. However, everyone of them would sneak away to the placer whenever he could. Whenever people needed extra help, they always thought of the Kirtley clan. Mary tutored their girls well in the art of cooking and housekeeping. While still in their teens two of the girls cooked all summer for the large crew of men at the placer.

Mary gracefully accepted Frank's resignation from her college plan. He was adamant in his refusal to go, while Jimmy packed his clothes and left. When Wade and Jimmy returned with stories of people and places they'd seen and parties they'd managed to attend, Frank just smiled, for envy them he did not.

When Charlie was eighteen it was his turn. The last boy and the fourth child, he was still small of stature but was wirery, strong and a goodlooking young man with dark, curly hair, blue eyes, and an easy smile. His wardrobe was meager but it contained enough good clothing so he would be able to attend school functions with no embarrassment. He chose a preparatory school in Deer Lodge, Montana, and attended that school one year. Then he transferred to the new University of Idaho at Moscow. Charlie loved school. With his quiet smile and friendly manner, he made friends with ease. The bull sessions at night always found Charlie in the middle recounting stories of ranch rodeos or the many escapades of his brothers and sisters.

When graduation finally came, the four-year students had dwindled to four, two men and two women. In the spring of 1896 Charlie received his degree in Civil Engineering. This was the first class to graduate from the University of Idaho at Moscow.

Each summer Charlie had gone home to help and he had been eager to be home with his family; but he never cared for ranching like Frank and Wade did. When he rode the fields and took the old trail to the mountain, his restless mind seemed to be seeking fulfillment. He pondered on this. He had first taken up engineering because of his love for mining. Somehow it seemed an empty goal as he gazed out across the mountains remembering the tales of hardship and the brothers and sisters lost because there was no doctor. His mother never ceased mourning her children and their wasted lives. Pioneers shouldn't have to be so helpless. He would go to medical school.

With the blessing of his family he enrolled in the Louisville Medical College at Louisville, Kentucky. After only one year he decided to transfer to the sprawling campus of Rush Medical College in Chicago. There he diligently applied himself to the rigorous routine of becoming a doctor. Letters sent home were full of the wonders of medicine, and he told them he had at last found contentment.

Charlie spent his internship at Cook County Hospital in Chicago, where poverty and disease were prevalent among the patients. Because of his eagerness to learn and his outstanding record, Dr. Coffee, a cancer specialist from Portland, Oregon, chose Charlie to be his junior partner. It was an excellent opportunity for Charlie, and located in the West, closer to home. They made their rounds each day at the hospital and examined and treated patients at the office. There were days when Charlie wondered if the whole world was afflicted with misery. Then he would think of his Idaho mountains and the excitement of watching for the golden nuggets to show. After working for Dr. Coffee for 18 months, he was walking down the long hospital corridor when he was summoned to the telephone. As he placed the receiver to his ear, he heard his mother's voice saying,

"Charlie, we need your skill and knowledge here at home. Nell's family is in serious trouble. Three days ago Bob was working night shift at the 'Queen of the Hills' Mill near Carmen, when a belt lacing came loose. It whipped around the corner of his jacket and pulled him into the fly wheel. They are sure he was pulled around several times until his body became lodged between the flywheel and the floor. It caused the machinery to stop and the lights to go out all over the mill. A man at the bunkhouse must have had a vivid dream because he jumped out of bed and yelled, 'Bob Walker is hurt.' The other men in the bunkhouse thought he was having a nightmare, but nevertheless they looked out the window to check. They rushed to the engine room, and found Bob's unconsciencious body on the floor. A rider was sent for the mine doctor and for Nell. Bob's chest was crushed, causing shallow breathing, while it seemed every bone the doctor touched was broken. He cut away the rest of Bob's tangled clothes from his body, washed the blood encrusted gravel and dirt from his face and body. Nell arrived within minutes of the doctor. Bob's condition was a great shock to her, but you know how fast she recovers from strain. In minutes she had men preparing him for the trip down the mountain. Jimmy and Wade are spelling her off and on round-the-clock nursing. Charlie, can you come home?"

Charlie left Portland and went to Salmon. When he saw what shape his brother-in-law was in, he again felt that grim challenge with death. He set bones, bound up broken ribs, stitched up long gashes, and administered medicine. The family pitted their strength against this adversary and Bob continued to improve. Word leaked out that Charlie was home, and his friends began calling him for emergencies and illnesses. He visited ranch houses, mines, and wood-camps. The more isolated the place, the more he realized the dire need for medical help. When he left Portland, Charlie had intended to stay for the length of his brother-in-law's illness. Now it was apparent that his work in Portland was finished. Charlie methodically checked the list of the mining camps, and chose Custer and vicinity as the area most in need of a doctor. At the age of 31, he moved to Custer in 1903. He rented a house and furnished it with furniture and office equipment.

Up to this time the only woman in Charlie's life had been his mother. The constant striving to keep ahead of his lessons had left little time for courting pretty girls. However, there had been occasions when he had accompanied ladies to different functions.

On impulse, he decided to attend the dance with a box social at midnight. As he strolled toward the Thompson Building, his feet quickened to the rhythm of the guitar and fiddle, played by his new friends George Coryall and Frank Coleman. As Charlie walked into the crowded dance hall, he stepped to one side of the door and idly watched the pleasure-loving dancers as they circled the floor. Among this laughing, happy crowd was a tall, slender redhead with snapping green eyes, a freckled face and saucy grin. As Charlie's eyes followed her around the floor, he noticed she was very young, but extremely self-assured with no trace of embarrassment as Charlie and another young man repeatedly cut in on her. The longer Charlie watched the more interested he was in this delightfully happy girl. As the music changed to a call dance of Tag Waltz, he tapped Charlie B. on the shoulder and waltzed away with Josephine Malm. Generally Josie felt very self-confident, but when the "Doctor" singled her out and danced with her several times, she became flustered and tongue-tied. Entertaining a 31 year old man-of-the-world was something new for a girl of 13 years.

At midnight Charlie Kirtley bid on Josie's boxed lunch and found a secluded corner of the hall where a chair served as a table. Josie spread the gay, printed tablecloth, and set out the picnic lunch of fried chicken, fresh baked bread, crisp watercress salad and sliced chocolate cake. After her initial embarrassment, Josie was soon chatting easily with Charlie telling him of her life in Custer and its parties of ice skating, taffy pulling, and picnics. When the music started up again, they put away the remainder of the lunch, folded the cloth and joined the group of dancers on the crowded floor.

The rest of the night Charlie skillfully kept Josie away from the stag line. As the Malms started to leave the dance, Charlie received permission to walk Josie home.

The full moon shone as they strolled along hand in hand. Charlie was less aware of the great difference in their ages as he told Josie of the years he had spent in colleges and how important education was to him. He told her that he even used his civil engineering knowledge when he operated because it helped him to lay out the area.

When they reached her door, Josie turned to thank him for the wonderful evening but found herself in a quandry. She had been speculating on what to call a doctor who obviously was interested in her. As she fumbled with

      "Thank you for the nice evening Dr. Kirtley -- no, I mean, Charlie."

He captured her hands and looking into her eyes, said,

      "Josie, never call me Dr. Kirtley. It sounds much too formal for the close friendship I hope we will soon have."

He smiled at her and exclaimed,

      "Really, I don't know what you are going to call me, as I refuse to let you call me Charlie. You might think you are talking to your other friend Charlie B."

The moon shone on Josie's face lighting up her mischievous grin as she said,

      "All right, I'll call you, Boy. Good night, Boy,"

she said as she disappeared into the house.

That was the beginning of their courtship. Dr. Kirtley treated patients in his office in their worn homes, in tents, sheep camps, mine shafts and sometimes on tables in saloons after a drunken brawl. He tried to keep his evenings free to continue the school lessons he was giving Josie at her home. He escorted her to all the social activities and many times at night they simply strolled along the roads and trails watching and studying the stars.

When it was time for Josie to graduate from the 8th grade, the new member of the school board, Charlie Kirtley, signed her diploma.

As the mines were closing down and work was scarce for the Malms, they made the heartbreaking decision to leave Custer and move to Challis to live with Josie's grandparents who owned a ranch. (This ranch is now part of the Floyd Bradbury ranch and this house and outbuildings can still be seen up in the Bradbury field.)

In Challis Josie's mother continued to take in washing, and was often engaged as a midwife. She was also a dressmaker. Josie and Charlie continued to correspond, and whenever he had an opportunity to visit her, he went to Challis. As each visit became more painful at parting, they set August 3, 1907 as their wedding date. Charlie left Custer at 4:00 A.M. on that day riding a horse and leading a saddle horse. He took the old toll road to Challis. At 10:00 A.M. thirty five year old Charlie and seventeen year old Josie were united in marriage at her grandparents' home. After the wedding breakfast, Charlie helped his new bride onto her mount for the trip to Custer.

As they rode along side by side, they happily planned their future. At noon they dismounted by a cool shaded spring and ate the delicious lunch Josie's mother had lovingly prepared for them.

Since Josie was not used to riding horseback, she was beginning to become bruised and sore from the jolting gait of her horse. At 4:00 o'clock she begged Charlie to stop, if only for a little while. He found it very hard to refuse his bride's wishes, especially since she was pale and tired, but he was an old hand at dealing with greenhorn horseback riders and knew he must not let her dismount. If anything they must speed up their journey. When he at last helped her down from her horse and carried her across the threshold of her new home, she summed up enough strength to give Charlie a ragged, lopsided grin to keep from crying from exhaustion.

So, the Kirtleys set up housekeeping in Custer. Their home had been a saloon in the upper part of town, but someone had moved it closer to the mill. The front room was Charlie's office, while the living room, bedroom and dining room were next to the kitchen. The Kitchen was down a step next to the long woodshed. The outdoor plumbing was behind this shed. Directly opposite the back door they had a well, equipped with a hand pump.

They were a happy couple. Josie was glad to be back in Custer. She loved being a doctor's wife and was very proud of him when he never turned away anyone day or night who needed his skills. When it was time for their baby to be born, Charlie was the proud father of the baby boy as well as the "doctor." They named their child Charles Gordon.

Charlie's love of mining had taken a backseat for a number of years. Now that he had a good practice, a wife and family, he again took up the pick and shovel whenever he could find the time. When Baby Gordon was only three months old, he put a pillow on his saddle against the saddle horn and cradled the baby there all the way up to the Kirtley claims on Bachelor mountain. When they reached their destination, he settled his family under a tree close by where he could visit with them and dig. (Speaking of these excursions Josie in later years would recall how no matter where Charlie chose to dig he always seemed to find gold. She said he would slowly shake the pan from side to side, and she would see a far away look come over his face. Momentarily the doctor was replaced by a little boy standing at his father's side looking for "color.")

Charlie, like his father, never gave up the dream of finding a strike. He grubstaked a few prospectors, investing large sums of money on the Bachelor mountain property. The claims also proved to be a place where he could relax and leave behind him the health problems of his neighbors and friends.

Gradually Custer was becoming a ghost town.. The men were slowly leaving as one by one the mines closed. The Kirtleys sadly boarded up their little home and moved to Salmon in 1910. Charlie had given some thought to moving to Leadore and had had a house built there. After carefully weighing all factors, they decided to settle in Challis instead.

The years there were very busy. Charlie had a practice that was demanding. He was truly a "horse and buggy" doctor, for ranches were far apart. Sometimes when he had stayed with a patient all night, he fell asleep as soon as he settled in the buggy; the horse would take him home.

The Kirtleys became the parents of three more children: Jimmy (named after Charlie's brother), Jack, and Charlotte. Charlie delivered them all. Charlotte was born at 7:30 a.m. and he walked the floor until 8:00 so he could go down town and tell all his friends he was the father of a baby girl.

Their large home was the scene of many parties. They enjoyed entertaining friends. They also made a home for any stray nephews or nieces who needed one.

As the family grew up and moved away, Charlie and Josie again sought after the refuge of Bachelor Mountain. Often times Charlie would go there by himself. He would work the claims during the day, then go down to Custer in the evenings. There he would visit and swap stories with Harry McClure, Ed Solomon, and other "gold-dreamers" who had not given up their town and were still prospecting claims. They would talk late into the night. These were some of Charlie's happiest days. He could forget time and troubles in the quiet ghost town of Custer. When he was rested and his strength renewed, he would again go home to his demanding practice.

On December 1, 1938, he was called across the river to set a broken leg for a lady patient. It was a difficult fracture and he was extraordinarily tired when he had set and cast it. As he slowly drove to town he felt a giant hand grab his heart, then a crushing pain surge down his arm. He stopped the car and leaned against the steering wheel, while the pain slowly ebbed away. But Charlie knew. . . .

When he arrived home he kept his terrible secret to himself. As he walked in the door Josie noticed his white, strained face. She dropped the plate she was carrying and pushed a chair toward him, exclaiming,

"Charlie, what is the matter, what happened?"
He quietly put his arm around her and patted her saying.
"I think I must have a touch of the flu. I believe I

will just lie down for a few minutes."
As he lay on the bed, he felt utterly exhausted and his medical knowledge told him he could very soon expect another attack. His mind drifted to his boyhood, manhood, and fatherhood. Lying there he decided he wouldn't have changed one thing if he had it to do over again.

When the old family clock melodiously started striking 10:00 he had the sickening awareness that his heart was malfunctioning. Josie saw the reflection of great pain in his white anguished face. She slipped to the floor and knelt by his side with her arms around him trying to hold him forever. But his life slowly drained away.

Little Charlie the milker, horse wrangler, cowboy, engineer, doctor and miner had traveled his last mile. He had earned his spurs.

Charles Kirtley, back row on the steps of the new University of Idaho at Moscow, Id. He was one of the first four graduates to graduate from the new university.

Members and friends of the Kirtley family: (top row) Joe Williams, Charlie Kirtley, (middle row) Nellie Kirtley, Hope McCalbel, Rose Stevens, Ettie Edwards, (front row) Thres McPherson, Mame McNab, Guy Edwards, Mam Edwards.

Dr. Charles Kirtley, Josie, Anna Malm (John Malm's wife) and Jack Kirtley, taken in front of a house on upper Main Street in Challis.

An older Doctor Kirtley; Dr. Kirtley standing with his new car.

Large log Malm home in a field know as the Floyd Bradbury field. Jose Malm and Charlie Kirtley were married in the parlor of this home August 3, 1907.

SHE WALKED A LONELY ROAD

The leaves were falling in 1897 when the stage bumped over the last stretch toward Challis with its low-built cabins and raw-lumber buildings huddled beneath the red bluff. As the wheels churned the dust into a cloud around the stage, Louise T. Treolor thought she had never seen such a desolate-looking place. The scrubby, twisted omnipresent sagebrush covered the landscape like a gray pall, and the cattle grazing among it made her idly wonder what they were finding to eat.

She leaned her head back against the seat, and with closed eyes recalled the events that had led up to this moment. She was thirty years old and wondered which circumstances to blame for this drastic change in her life. It was easy to recall the splendid home with servants to anticipate every whim. Her sisters and brothers, Willie and Edward, were part of it -- also expensive boarding schools, elaborate clothing, prancing horses to drive and ride. Her family had influence on county, state and federal levels. In 1885 at eighteen, she had worn a changeable blue taffeta dress with French ecru lace freely framing the neckline and tops of the sleeves to Grover Cleveland's inaugural ball. To the second inaugural ball she had worn a creamy white satin gown. She had received the pleasure of being invited to the functions, as well as, being asked to give a piano recital for them. Then her thoughts drifted to the heartaches all the girls suffered in the south with the young men leaving their poverty-stricken homes as soon as they were old enough to strike out for themselves -- and the gradual process of the girls becoming "old maids." This last circumstance, she decided, had finally driven her away from home to this raw, little town. Lou leaned forward when she felt the stage driver pull the horse to a stop in from of the tiny station.

The stage door was eagerly pulled open by her brother Edward, who saw his sister as he remembered her. Resembling their mother, she was tall, small-boned, with light brown hair, blue eyes and an attractive smile. When he had helped her from the carriage, Ed noticed she still walked with proud grace and spoke in a low, well-controlled voice which easily disclosed her early training. Billy, also took part in the happy reunion, and the boys collected her luggage. Then the three Trelors walked next door from the stage station and rented rooms at the Challis House. After refreshing themselves they took Louise on a tour of the town.

Next morning Ed and Louise completed the trip to Bayhorse where Ed was working. As they approached the bottom of Main Street, Louise asked Ed to stop the wagon while she looked over her new town.

"Why, Ed!" she exclaimed,

"It looks like this little town has been pushed down into the bottom of these steep walls. Look! Every available inch of space is taken up with cabins, tents or lean-tos. Where in the world will you turn around?"

He chucked,

"Well, if you are in a hurry, I guess you could turn around anyplace. Of course, you might run down a few tents, but seriously, it is necessary to go up to the mill to turn around."

Activity was lively in the streets with dogs, teams and people. For good measure most of the children played in the streets because it was the only place wide enough to play games. Men were everywhere. She correctly guessed that several buildings where men were congregated were saloons -- there were 13 of them.

After her brother found space in the small cabin for Louise's boxes and trunks, she hung up her traveling dress, selected one for housework, shook out a crisp gingham apron, and was ready to begin her new life.

Bayhorse was a friendly town. "Miss Lou," as Ed called her from habit of long ago, became acquainted with the ladies. A small group of them resented her southern breeding and lovely manners, her rich clothing and soft speech. Spitefully they accused her of "putting on airs."

At first she attended the social functions with Ed. However, she was soon seriously considering marriage to a tall, dark, handsome freighter called Joseph P. Short. He seemed to admire her maturity and considered the three year's difference in age a distinct advantage. On March 1898 they were united in marriage at Bayhorse with Nora Fouglar and Gus Sergeant as their witnesses. Guy Foster, minister of the Congregational Church of Challis, performed the ceremony. The usual dinner, dance and celebration followed the wedding. Even the kids celebrated by staging a charivari -- banging on cans, buckets, and pans. Joe finally opened the door and tossed a gold nugget to each participant.

The Shorts lived in Bayhorse until Joe filled his wood contract. Their next move was to Custer where he again banked out wood. He was developing a bad habit of being frequently absent from home for days at a time. Louise's pride would not allow her to question him, while maintaining an attitude to the world that he was away on business. Until the night of his absence, she had never been alone in her life. She often asked Mrs. Johnson if little Lillie could come in for the evening and spend the night with her. As Joe's absences became more frequent, many times Louise would be without food. Her proud, lonely figure would be seen dressed in her immaculate dark cashmere suits with frilly white blouses strolling along in the evening. Then she would knock on one of her friend's doors. Since the family would usually be eating, with warm western hospitality she was always asked to join them. On one of her brother's visits to Custer, he found her with no money to pay the rent, so he put in a supply of groceries and commissioned a stone mason to build her a one-room, rock building high on the hill overlooking the town. It was small with barely room for the fireplace at one end, table, bed and a few chairs. But it was cool in summer and was snug in the winter. The overflowing, cool, spring by the side of her house furnished her with good drinking water. Her one lack was her husband's companionship.

During the time she spent in Custer and later on when she lived in Challis, Miss Lou wrote glowing letters to her sister Lucy, telling her of her wonderful marriage. Living in the remote mountains had made it difficult for Louise to visit her family; however, she was a good correspondent and derived some comfort from that. On the afternoon of November 13, 1904, the stage driver from Challis knocked on her door and stood hesitantly on the stoop. When she asked him to enter, he rolled the hat in his hand from side to side and told her he had some very bad news for her. As gently as he could, he said that Willie was dead -- either by his own hand or by murder. She stared at him in horror, unable to comprehend the terrible news. Realizing she would never see her dashing older brother smile again, she sat down in shock. Gradually she made up her mind to leave. The driver made arrangements to carry her boxes and trunks on the stage, and without a second glance Louise left Custer. It had been a trying experience, and she had no fond memories to make her want to stay.

Louise moved in with her sister-in-law, Lizzie, and helped her with the lonely business of learning to live without Willie. It was a sad time in her life, nevertheless, she enjoyed the warm hospitality of the Treolor home. After several weeks, Joe showed up at the ranch and casually mentioned he had a winter job on the Small brothers' ranch, which also furnished a small cabin for them to live in (this is the present Lynn Wilson ranch). With reluctance Louise rejoined her husband. Gone was the rapture of their first carefree wedding days. She no longer believed in him and was daily apprehensive that he would soon be gone again. When the leaves started to show on the trees and the grass began to green-up, Joe left under the pretense of going to Forney looking for a wood contract. She received a little money from her parents estate. In desperation she caught the stage to Forney where her brother Ed was managing the stage station. She finally told him of her plight and enlisted his aid finding her errant husband. Since Ed had dealt with a continual stream of men going and coming from the mining and wood camps, he had insight into the nomadic life of many of them. After hearing Louise's story, he classed Joe with them and offered to let her ride the stage to Salmon to Joe's friend's home. Courageously she went to the McKinney's home. After the evening meal, Louise asked Mr. McKinney if he had heard from Joe. His face was full of sympathy as he quietly told her,

> "Louise, he was here three days ago and told me he would not be returning to Challis. I asked him about you, and he said he had no wife. I'm sorry, Louise. He was a fine young man, but I think we will have to attribute his behavior to that Western sickness, 'gold.'"

When Louise boarded the stage for Forney, gone was the gentle woman who had been reared to respect men. She became a man-hater. Arriving at Forney, Louise poured out her heartbroken story. Ed offered her a home and a job cooking and helping with the station. She remained there for three years. One evening Fred Albeitz was telling Ed about his property in Challis. Fred said he had squatter's rights on a 15 acre piece of property on the Challis Creek road. It had been tied up in title dispute for sometime as Ferdinand Klug had files on forty acres under the Homestead Act which had included his tract. Now Fred's title was clear, and he was anxious to sell it. Ed agreed to lend Louise the $349 it would take to buy it. At last she had a home of her own. The property had been built for a brewery, used for that purpose for three years and leased to Dr. Cutter for the County poorhouse. Next it had served as a temporary school house. Fred told her the rock work had been done by a fine stonemason from Germany. The work on the deep-set windows and doorways, plus the fireplace showed his fine talent.

Ed found someone to watch over the station and helped Louise move into her new home. With the money she had saved at Forney and her pitiful small inheritance, she hired a carpenter to build partitions dividing the house into four rooms. She also engaged him to build roofs over the old mash pits in the backyard, converting them into chicken coops. When the outbuildings were finished, she commissioned him to add two log rooms to the north side for rental. She rented them for many years. With two dozen chickens happily clucking and scratching in the new clean straw of their new coops, Louise soon had more eggs than she could use, so she traded the excess eggs for milk and cream. Next she wrote her sister and told her she was no longer Louise Short, but Louise Treolor (a name she kept until her death).

Within a month a fright attendant backed his delivery wagon up to her door and asked her where she would like her new piano placed? Her sister had sent it when she found Louise had a home of her own where she could give piano lessons. In a few weeks, her appointment book was filled; she was financially independent.

Louise bought a light buggy and a little mare she called Bessie. She became a familiar figure driving the country side with her dog trotting along behind.

One day after a long day of teaching pupils scales, chords, and melodies she heard a knock on the door. When she opened it there stood Joe, standing in the sun; handsome, with a devil-may-care look, he stood hat in hand. Her first impulse was to rush into his strong familiar arms, but the heartaches and stories of his indiscretions had reached her ears. In a cold voice she asked,

"What do you want?"

This was not the reception Joe had expected. Not giving him a chance to talk, she said,

"I am expecting a pupil here at the house, but I have a few things I want to say to you. Would you mind going for a walk?"

Joe immediately felt at ease and blithely helped her on with her coat. As they walked down Challis Creek Road to the fork, Joe tried to make his conversation sound as if he had never been gone. Louise stopped and looked him in the eyes.

"Joe, you were the dearest person on earth to me. I walked and rode many miles looking for you. I spent many days and nights hungry because you took what little money I had, and I have cried oceans of tears. I even kept a place set for you, covered with a white linen cloth for many months, so when you came home you would know how much I loved you. Now you have nothing left. You rode the high road and left me the crumbs. I have made a life for myself. Don't look back Mr. Short. You are standing where this road divides. It is symbolic. Our lives are now divided."

These were the last words Joe heard Louise speak.

After this walk with Joe, she seldom spoke of him again. She continued to busy herself with a large garden from which she preserved the excess for her winter food. She formed the habit of going to some of the pupils homes to give their lessons. It was a way of visiting and keeping in touch with the town. Such a pupil was Violet Woodman, who recounted memories of Miss Lou in a letter.

"Miss Lou was a romantic figure to me. She had 'things' and was so accomplished in a way that no one else in Challis was. I suppose she was the first 'lady' I ever came in contact with. How she ever managed to live with no income is just a mystery to me. Of course, she died practically penniless, and her treasures were sold at county auctions. Two paintings were bought by our family -- one by mother and one by Edna McGown. Ours was bought for a quarter. As I remember Miss

Lou, she was a tall woman, and she wore her suits regally. She would be fashionable by today's standards. The high-necked blouses were worn with a large brooch or else she wore this pin on a velvet ribbon around her neck. When she asked me to call her 'Miss Lou', she said, 'I am Louise Treolor to acquaintances, but Miss Lou to my friends.' I took lessons from her. Her poor hands had started to become deformed from arthritis. The only reason I had for taking lessons or owning a piano was my grandmother's determination to help Miss Lou be independent by having a profession. My grandfather was coaxed into buying the piano -- a Brinkerhoff from Chicago and shipped on wagon from Mackay. I have dear memories of going to see Miss Lou and having her tell my fortune. I loved every moment of the fortune because she had a way of saying things, making you think you were in some sort of conspiracy with her. Her charge was 25 cents. Of course her fortunes were happy ones and what I wanted to hear. She'd twinkle when she went into her little rhyme about, 'You'll be very happy and old as you please, have plenty of money and live at your ease.'

    Other girls in later times had Margaret Mitchell's 'Gone With The Wind' to compare people to. I had Miss Lou. She was a character right out of Miss Mitchell's book. She had been a 'Southern Belle' in North Carolina. After listening to her girlhood stories, I could easily picture her with servants deferring to her, a picture hat, ringlets, and the whole gracious manner of a true lady. Her favorite piece of music was 'Camptown Races' and she played it with a verve and style never to be equaled by any jazz-time great. She was an 'experience' -- a dashing figure going her lonely way so far away from her real home. In later years her home was quite unkempt because of her inability to keep it up, but it still had charm with her beautiful wall screen and a few elegant pieces of furniture. It impressed me. Challis was quite primitive in many ways. The so called "niceties" hadn't gotten to the community yet in the early 1900's. Everything different was suspect (sort of) and she had so many "differences" from the ordinary housewife that by some she was regarded as strange. The poor lonely lady with none of her kin to visit. My last visit with Miss Lou was just before I left for California in 1927. I never saw her again, but I mourned when I heard of her death.

As ever, Violet Woodman"

Through the years Louise received fashionable clothes from relatives in the South; and a few years after she had purchased her home, she used some of her carefully saved money to make a trip back to her former home. Whether she found conditions so changed or whether there was no place there for her, she never divulged. On her return trip she brought with her a number of Carolina Poplars which she planted along side of her house and lined her property with them. long after her death the trees remained -- mute evidence of the love she had for her birthplace. (Lloyd Reed cut down the last lone tree in 1975.)

Miss Lou had become a town "character." It became the thing for young people to have her tell their fortunes. (It was encouraged by parents who felt the 25 cents would help her maintain her financial dignity). Eventually she was teaching music to children of children she had taught.

The only concession she ever made to living alone was to ask her brother for a pistol which she kept on her bedside table. Occasionally she used it. A group of boys decided on a "chickerree" with her plump pullets as the main course. As they slipped into the coop, the door hinge squeaked. Instantly bullets strayed the door, pinning the unwelcome visitors in the lice-infested chicken coop. When she took time to reload, they made their escape.

She was thin and slight of stature, but she had a will of iron. When she felt she had been wronged, she took the matter into her own hands. Such was the case when the dispute over the the boundary line between hers and the Chivers property was settled. She said the strong, new, well-braced wire fence had not been put on the proper line. By dark of night she systematically sawed off a post or two every night, bracing them with a scab of lumber. The night she finished cutting into the last post, she pulled the scabs from each stump. When the Chivers family milked their cow next morning, the new fence was lying flat on the ground. Rather than cause her anymore trouble, a new fence was placed on the line she indicated.

When Miss Lou was no longer able to hold the lines to drive her mare, she sold her to a friend. Now she traveled about town, (generally at dusk) carrying a coal-oil lantern with half the chimney painted red so that it would not reflect her. Always her old dog faithfully trotted by her side. She usually had a pail of eggs which she was exchanging or else she carried vegetables.

She also developed a habit of smoking a small delicate cigar called cigarillos. If someone came to her house, and she had forgotten to hide the evidence, she would exclaim, "Oh! My friend has left his cigar again." She also kept a jug of wine for a special occasion or with her dinner.

Her only character flaw was her severe hatred of men who had been her husband's friends. One by one these men died, and each time she held a night-wake with a cigarillo smoking on the ashtray and a jug of wine handy while she played all the songs she ever knew, starting with "Camptown Races," and ending with "Old Black Joe." Now and then the renters would hear her say, "Well, I outlasted that old so and so!"

Even with the neighbors helping her out, she was forced to accept county aid by 1937. For the first two months her pension was $18 a month. Then it was raised to $23 a month from March 22, 1937 to December 12, 1940 she survived on a total of $851. Then the county appointed Dora West to take care of her. Louise still treasured her independence, and would not allow Dora to stay all night. On the morning of December 11, 1940, when Dora came to start her chores for the day, she found Miss Lou in a semiconscious state. With a weak wave of her hand, Louise indicated she did not need any help. Then she closed her eyes, sighed and quietly ceased breathing.

When the county started to clear her account, they found she had a bank account of $278 -- saved so she would not have to be buried "on the county." They settled her small store account of $166.90 and a drug store bill for $12.91, leaving $178 to pay for her own burial. They sold her home for taxes of $316, and listed her pitifully few possessions for auction. Friends bought them in memory of her. They were all that remained of a strong spirit who had asked no quarter and had given none. She had walked her lonely road with quiet dignity and fierce pride.

Louise Treolor (left) was reared in Charlotte, North Carolina.

Miss Lou at her home in Challis, with her firend Mrs. Carpenter. (Bottom) Miss Lou dressed to go to a pupil's home to teach music.

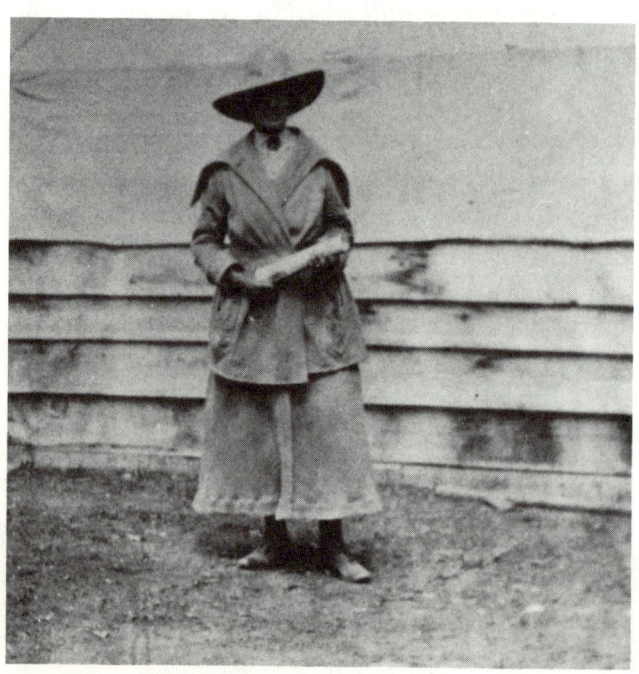

Mrs. Della McGown and granddaughter, Violet Woodman. Mrs. McGown befriended "Miss Lou" and engaged her to teach Violet piano lessions -- Mrs. Lou's only form of income.

SHE LIVED IN GOD'S DOMAIN

Slender brownhaired Edna McGown, former Custer Museum owner and co-author of two books say,

"My father was one of 12 children, who was raised by a childless aunt and uncle, and loved him as a son. They gave him the advantage of a good education. He left their home for a banking job in Denver, Colorado. But the big outdoors had a firm hold on him. When he heard of storekeeping job in Wyoming, he leaped at the chance to live in a frontier town. From there it only took him until he heard travelers talking about Valley Creek Mine in a little known town called, Stanley, Idaho to be on the trail."

She continues,

"So, my parents, 'Tink' and Ellen Neice packed their gear in a wagon with my three year old brother, Rupert. They traveled through the unbelievably hot desert of Utah and arrived at the top of Galena Summit in early summer. After the scorched land they had just traveled, the view of the Sawtooth Valley of lush green grass, high mountains and evergreen trees took a life-long hold on them.

When they pulled into the 'Nip and Tuck' station, they found the mid-wife, Mollie Paul, the manager. This was a happy coincidence because there was no place for a pregnant woman at the mine, so mother stayed there. I was born November, 1906.

The main venture was unsuccessful, but the beautiful land was waiting to be claimed. The Nieces homesteaded 160 acres of meadowland.

This was the first home I remember -- a two room cabin on this land. While we could have lived off the land by selling hay and a few cows, it still took cash-money to pay taxes and the proving-up fee. Money was something we had very little of. One of my aunts knew how the money situation was at our home and wrote, informing father there was plenty of work in Spokane, Wa. Leaving us his only mode of transportation, an old white saddle horse, my father walked all the way from Stanley to Spokane. He sent us money to live on and to pay the bills, saving enough to see us through another year."

Edna was seven years old when they left the ranch behind, and moved to Stanley where her father leased a grocery store and became the postmaster.

In this wild country there was no school, and Edna and Rupert were school age. Mrs. Josephine Thompson, a teacher turned rancher's wife, offered to take the two Merrit and the two Niece children into her home. The four children lived with John and Josephine Thompson for six months.

Edna recalled,
> "She set up a school room in one side of her 12'x14' livingroom with our little desks, blackboards, maps and her own desk. She held regular classes, eight hours a day, five days a week, with all required subjects. Friday afternoons were special Thinking back on those times I know our teacher was very modern. She allowed us freedom to be creative. We became artists, musicians, toe dancers, or maybe we just had spelling bees.
>
> She also taught us to be mannerly; how to set tables; how to entertain guests; and to be independent in our thinking.
>
> She managed privacy for our bedrooms by draping sheets across the middle of the 12'x14' bedroom. We three girls slept in one bed on our side The Thompson's bed was in the other section. Rupert's bedroom was in a colder room. After supper Mrs. Thompson always put two large smooth rocks in the oven to heat during the evening. When it was bedtime, she wrapped those heavy rocks in towels and placed them in the bottom of Rupert's bed. They always stayed warm until morning.
>
> Our evenings were fun. After the chores of wood, and water getting and the dishes were done, we played hide and seek or sat around the table and played games. There were evenings when we all cut rags for bright rugs, and were allowed to braid them."

The next year a school district had been formed in Stanley, so we kids stayed home and attended from there.

Wintertime in Stanley Basin often brings severe cold weather. The temperature can easily drop to 50 below zero. On such a day Edna says,
> "Rupert and I left school wrapped up in heavy clothes, overshoes on our feet, and warm mittens on our hands. Stocking caps with long tails wrapped around and around our heads left only our eyes showing. It's a good thing Dad told us not to stop NO MATTER WHAT! That mile and one-half seemed a hundred miles. The cold seemed to pull at us and through our clothes. It

made me so tired. I just sat down contented to stay. No doubt my brother was just as cold and tired as I was, but he had the good sense to grab me, shake me, and make me walk. When we neared the school, we saw the door fly open and Mrs. Thompson ushered us in and helped us remove our coats and boots and had us sit by the roaring fire."

Edna graduated from the eighth grade when she was 13 years old. Mrs. Thompson had allowed Edna to progress at her own rate of learning. Therefore, at the end of the term, she might have completed her grade or be halfway through the next. The following fall she picked up where she left off. Edna says,

"I never was in a real grade. Just in between. When my teacher thought I was ready, she asked the superintendent of schools to come to Stanley and give me my eighth grade examination, which I passed."

During her high school years Edna had to board away from home at Challis, and it was a lonesome time for her. While attending high school she started to date "Tuff" McGown, a young man who had been raised in the goldmining town of Custer. After it became a ghost town, his family moved to Challis.

Edna recalls,

"Tuff acquired that nickname when he was two years old and must have felt bound to live up to it, for he did some hair raising things. He drilled a peephole in the dash of his Model T Ford so he could see to drive the full length of Main Street with no apparent operator behind the wheel. When he came to the end of the street, he shot up and turned the corner. Needless to say he was considered "wild" by his parents. With me he was gentle and kind.

I was looking for another place to board the winter I was 18, and a senior in high school. Tuff's folks were planning to go to California for the winter. He was going to batch it. It just seemed like a good time to get married. I quit school, and we were married November 25, 1924. We had nothing; not even a towel or a sheet. When the senior McGowns left, we lived in their home that winter. Meantime we worked on the house they had given us for a wedding present. When spring came, we had enough household wares put together to move in."

Even though Custer was a ghost town, it was where Tuff had been raised, and it was still home to him. He convinced Edna they could make a living there placer mining. The McGowns moved in late spring. For the next nine years they lived there both summers and winters. Each fall they laid in supplies for all winter. For extra cash Tuff ran a trap line. They had chinked up the cracks in one of the abandoned log houses and banked up around the outside of the bottom logs. Edna muses,

> "The snow came in mounds, snowing sometimes days at a time, but we had a shed full of dry pitchy wood, and we were fixed up cozy. Not once did I ever mind being snowed in. Occasionally we would snowshoe to Sunbeam, ten mile away for mail, news and some small items we might need."

During those nine years the McGowns became the parents of three children, Arthur, Adelaide, and Edna Mae. Two of the children were September babies, so they were able to get to a doctor. Edna Mae was delivered by her Grandmother and a nurse. When little Arthur was school age his mother taught him his first grade.

When all of the children were ready for school, the McGowns moved to Challis in winter, but continued to placer mine in the summer. At times when they needed more money than the mine produced, Tuff worked for the Forest Service. The family followed the same pattern until the children grew up and married.

As is true of all families, the McGowns were not without their sorrows. Their only son was killed by a belly-dump in 1956 when he was just 29 years old; leaving a wife and small child.

More and more of the artifacts of the ghost town was being lost. In desperation, Edna and Tuff decided to buy the old school house where Tuff and all of the Custer kids had gone to school, and turn it into a museum.

They started it in 1960 and managed it until 1966. It was a satisfying, successful adventure. Each year added excitement as they searched for things to add to their collection.

As more and more visitors streamed through the doors, the McGowns realized the upkeep and expense was going to become prohibitive for them. Also at the time, Tuff's health had started to fail. In 1966, when the Forest Service made them an offer, they accepted with the stipulation it would always be open to the public.

The same drive to preserve the yarns and facts being lost by death of the oldtimers caused Edna and Tuff to co-author a book with Esther Yarber called, "Land of the Yankee Fork." It describes in detail the pioneer days.

After the sale of the museum, the McGowns moved to a place more accessible in winter on a scenic overcrop of the Salmon River. There they built a home tastefully furnished throughout with antique oak furniture. They moved into their completed home on a typical golden fall day in October. Two months later, Edna lost her "wild" companion. Tuff suffered a fatal heart attack.

Edna says,

"Idaho has offered to me its mountains to live in, its creeks to fish, and its 'shiny' metal to feed my family. I have been privileged.

One time while sitting in a wagon on top of a summit, as we stopped to give the horses a 'breather,' my dad said it all in one sentence: 'In land like this, can we be very far from God?'"

Wedding picture of Tuff and Edna.

(Top) Family group (Bottom) Niece Stanley home in Winter.

(Top) General Custer Mill while it was in good working order.
(Bottom) A picture of a tired old Mill taken in 1930.

McGown Museum; Tuff; (bottom) Edna and Rupert; Edna.

Custer as it was when "Tuff" was growning up.

IF YOU CAN SEE THROUGH THE MISTS

The sun of Custer shimmers on grass and trees
As it has for one hundred years, it's true
The woods and willows and whispered breeze
Of a mining town they knew.

Through mists of time and backward glance
Rekindled in our beings
Were cabins built, and past romance
The busy Custer springs.

Three thousand voices echoed brave halloos
Over campfires, tended all night long
Back-breaking toil, some dreams came true
For many . . . a broken song.

Where magpies fly and bluebirds build
And badgers heap their mounds
There once were roads with grades uphill
Through this lonely Custer town.

And if you walk through pines thereabouts
Hear hushed and listening things
And see the crimson-sided trout
By his bubbled-circled rings, and

Hear a lone coyote, a callin' to his fate
The fact is here,
They no longer fear
The booted man and his mate.

You can hear the beat of the miners' feet
And the swish of a skirt in the dew
And can almost see, a bent Chinese
On a path where flowers grew.

If you stand still and listen
You can hear their shouts of joy
As they strode the path, down the mountain trail
From the mighty "Lucky Boy."

The booted feet, these hills they trod
Those mining volunteers

They've passed beyond and into mists
Of "the Custer Pioneers."

The ring of voices, kids large and small
Pig-tailed and some with freckles
The split-out seams, and patched blue-jeans
Fish poles, and trout all speckled.

The "Yankee Fork" splashes down the rocks
As one hundred years gone past
Now the banks are uncluttered, a Paradox
Of log and board held fast.

Their cabins gone, squirrels chatter on
Where chimneys filled the air
And the pioneers' town of you and me
Is a shrouded thoroughfare.

And like a fortress, against the rot
A school house regal in it's stance
Remembers pressure from cabins squat
Against its' painted contenance.

But most of all, you can hear the call
Hobnails on the old boardwalks
The rutted roads, the mules' heavy loads
Passed down from the burdened ox.

And all the after-bearers see
Are sagebrush, rocks, and paths unsure
But they stand guard to protect the past
Of people who are no more.